B AND OLD
BEAUTIFUL

Judi Dains

BOLD AND BEAUTIFUL

ARTFUL QUILTS FROM JUST ONE FABRIC

Martingale®
& COMPANY

CREDITS

President & CEO • Tom Wierzbicki

Editor in Chief • Mary V. Green

Managing Editor • Tina Cook

Technical Editor • Nancy Mahoney

Copy Editor • Durby Peterson

Design Director • Stan Green

Production Manager • Regina Girard

Illustrator • Laurel Strand

Cover & Text Designer • Shelly Garrison

Photographer • Brent Kane

MISSION STATEMENT

Dedicated to providing quality products
and service to inspire creativity.

Bold and Beautiful: Artful Quilts from Just One Fabric
© 2009 by Judi Dains

That Patchwork Place® is an imprint of
Martingale & Company®.

Martingale & Company
20205 144th Ave. NE
Woodinville, WA 98072-8478 USA
www.martingale-pub.com

Printed in China
14 13 12 11 10 09   8 7 6 5 4 3 2 1

Library of Congress Cataloging-in-Publication Data
Library of Congress Control Number: 2008054605

ISBN: 978-1-56477-892-5

DEDICATION

I first acknowledge and dedicate my talents to God, who has led me and granted me all my inspiration. Without His small still voice of encouragement, I would never have had this opportunity. Along the way, He placed all I needed in my path—family and friends who encouraged me as I struggled with believing in myself.

I dedicate this book to my family members, my mom and dad, sisters and brothers, who graciously received gifts of love from me that, at times, were pretty darned imperfect. You overlooked the little tangles, holes, and imperfections, and each time I gave, I got more in return.

Blessings back to all of you.

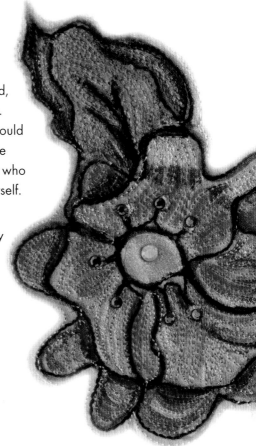

ACKNOWLEDGMENTS

Thanks to:

- Sue Rhorke, my traveling buddy, supporter, and encourager. I can still hear you saying, "Write the book." So here's to you, Suzzie. Thanks for the vote of confidence, years of great laughter, and friendship.

- My quilt guilds; you raised me above what I thought I deserved and encouraged, taught, and accepted me and my unconventional style.

- Judges; you directed me with corrections when I needed improvement and encouraged me in my artistic abilities. You do make a positive difference.

- My Christian friends who prayed and spoke words of love and hope. You are the glue that holds me together.

- My students, who lifted me up and saw what I didn't see in myself. You taught me to move forward by making me feel that I had something to offer. I will always teach you what I know.

- My husband, Jim, who spent many boring hours downstairs alone while I was in my studio working. Thank you for those hours you sacrificed to allow me to get this book in order.

- My daughter, Cindy, and granddaughter, Grace, who live near but seemed far, because Grandma was busy working on her book. We squeezed in every moment we could. Thank you for encouragement and understanding.

- My son, Brian, and his family. Thank you for your excitement and faith in me.

- Patti Henderson, owner of Cabin Fever Quilt Shop in Auburn, California. I won't forget the day I was teaching this technique and you said, "Stop. Go home and write the book." I did. I appreciate your excitement and enthusiasm.

- Martingale & Company. From the first call from Karen Soltys, who brought the good news, you were all delightful and encouraging! Nancy Mahoney, thank you for the many hours you spent diligently going over my manuscript to make it just right. Your expertise is greatly appreciated. To everyone on staff, thank you. Your expertise, advice, correction, and knowledge have made my dream come true.

I have been blessed by all of you, so I send back a double portion of blessings to you.

CONTENTS

WHERE ARTIST AND QUILTMAKER MEET

When one is raised in Erie, Pennsylvania, the elusive sun is a thing to seek and appreciate. At age 14, I was aware of the power of a beautiful suntan and wanted to get a head start on all my friends. I would usually start working on my tan in April, when most of the time it was still quite chilly. Yet the sun was so yummy and inviting that I'd set up my lounge chair in the middle of our large lawn and wrap myself in a heavy blanket, waiting for that perfect moment when the clouds would roll past and grant me my time in the sun. Underneath the blanket I'd be wearing my bathing suit. When the clouds moved away and the sun revealed its rays, I'd throw off the blanket and soak up all I could get. When the clouds rolled over the sun again, I'd get under cover until the next bit of sun peeked through. It was during this time of my life that I became a cloud gazer.

I think we've all experienced cloud gazing at one time or another. But for me, it became a hobby of sorts. On long road trips my family would make a passing-the-time game of it. This past year on our way to Arizona, my husband and I both saw Jack Nicholson's shining face in the clouds! Admittedly, it does take imagination. That's where your inner artist comes in. You merely need to train your eyes and your imagination—and then put what you saw on canvas.

Recently I've discovered objects in my batik fabrics just as I've done in cloud formations. So, just as the yummy sun warmed my body, the yummy batiks warm my heart.

I never saw myself as an artist—probably because of my own preconceived idea of what an artist was and did. Over the years, many people have suggested that I was an artist, but I didn't see it until I thought about it for a while. I concluded that since my quilts are my own designs and they're considered art quilts, maybe all those people were right.

After all, artists and quiltmakers are both creative people. We both speak from our hearts and with our hands. So, this is where the artist meets the quiltmaker—a place I want to take you, through this book.

THE DAWNING LIGHT

The light dawned for me when I was able to look at a piece of batik fabric and see *beyond the fabric*. Filled with outside-the-box ideas and creative thinking, this book will help you enhance many of your skills, including quilting and artistic abilities that may be hidden within. I will also introduce you to new ideas to help develop your creative talents so that you too can see beyond the fabric. This book will take you to a place where every person in a classroom can start with the same fabric, apply her own artistic interpretation, and create a work with its own unique identity in the art world—where artist and quiltmaker meet. Through this process, I hope you, too, will experience the dawning light as you develop your creative abilities and passion.

Soon you'll understand the meaning of what I call *hidden treasures*. The first hidden treasure is the artist in each of you. I love to proclaim myself a quiltmaker. However, the desire of my heart is to be called an artist.

Now, there are other hidden treasures also—these are the ones I find in batik or hand-dyed fabric. In the sections that follow, I'll share the process of finding these hidden treasures with you. Don't worry—the process is understandable and easy. If you're like me, as we go through the process you'll open your eyes to new possibilities and develop your creativity, bringing out the artist within. And, we'll walk down a path that will delight you each step of the way.

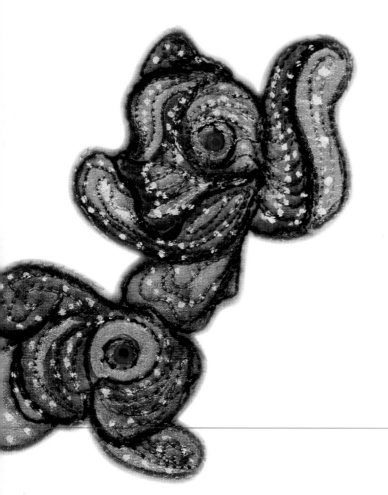

STARTING THE ARTISTIC PROCESS

Are you ready to grow as an artist? For the projects in this book, you'll begin the creative process by choosing the right fabric and then seeing beyond the fabric to find hidden treasures. Once you've found objects in the fabric that jump out at you, you'll outline the objects, first with a permanent marker and then with heavy thread. Next you'll add borders—or not, it's your choice—and you'll be well on your way to creating an art quilt!

CHOOSING FABRICS WISELY

Bring on the batiks—the artist is in the building!

Choosing the right fabric is the first step to success. If you choose the wrong type of batik or hand-dyed fabric, or if you select a fabric with strong color transition (what I call a color wave), you will be pushed to stretch yourself before you even begin. So, listen carefully and choose wisely.

There is a delicious array of batik and hand-dyed fabrics on the market, not to mention fabric that you may dye yourself. (If you're a fabric dyer, lucky you. You already have a head start on the creative path.) The fabric you choose will determine the outcome of your quilt. Because the quilts in this book are based on one main fabric or a whole-cloth center, the choices of fabric will be much easier to determine. I categorize my batiks using just a few terms.

FABRICS TO AVOID

These fabrics are difficult to use for various reasons and should be avoided.

Muddy Fabrics

Muddy fabrics are muted and lackluster, and they do not make a good background for the painting we'll be doing. On these fabrics, the paints become lost and you might find yourself overpainting to compensate for the muddy colors.

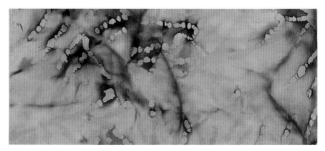

Muddy fabrics are dull and boring.

Fabrics That Are Too Dark

A color wave that's too dark would also be difficult to work with, because the fabric's darkness drowns out the paints. Even light-colored paints would get swallowed up in the darkness of the fibers. Deep greens, blues, and reds fall into this category. If you've found that a fabric you've already chosen is too dark, here's a tip to make it work: dot the dark fabric with white paint or ink after the first layer of paint dries. The white paint will be visible on the dark fabric and perk it up a bit.

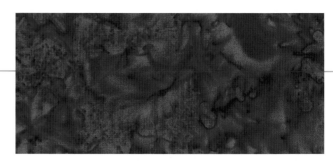

Fabrics that are too dark are tricky to paint.

Stamped Batiks

This type of batik has a ready-made design that takes away from your creativity, unless you use the ready-made design in part of your plans. I included stamped batiks in some of my quilts when the batiks provided a design element that I could work into my plans.

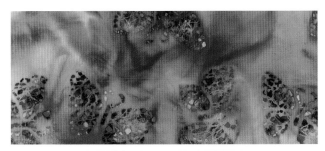

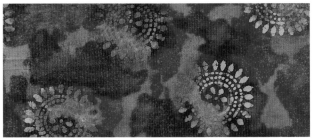

Stamped batiks can be problematic.

Overdyed Pattern

These can be subtle and may not be noticeable until you put the fabric on the design wall and look through a camera lens or reducing glass. The overdyed pattern will then pop out and you will have a difficult time hiding it.

An overdyed pattern can overwhelm your design.

Overly Small Pattern

If the fabric has a small-scale, overcrowded, unidentifiable, or unreadable pattern, it could be difficult to use because the closeness of the pattern might make your quilt look too cluttered. However, I love small patterns if they have enough color change. This can give you a little flower-bouquet or flower-garden look.

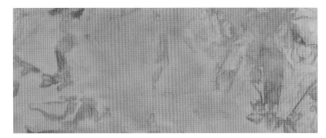

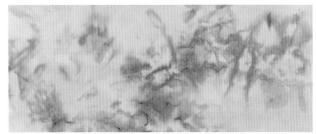

Fabrics with an overly small pattern scale can create a disorganized look.

Reducing Glass

A reducing glass looks like a magnifying glass but works in the opposite way. It makes objects that are nearby appear as though they're far away. The lens of a camera or a peephole such as the one you would use in your front door can also be used as a reducing glass.

FABRICS TO LOOK FOR

Look for the following types of fabrics, which will inspire you and get the creative juices flowing.

Batiks with Large-Scale Patterns

Now, these I love, because of their large splashes of color. They have so much design potential. The large splashes of pattern and color are great for small quilts because they can be offset for that perfect imbalance that's desirable in so many artistic paintings. For larger quilts, these batiks give you a large-scale design pattern that gives proportion to the quilt.

Batiks with large-scale patterns have lots of design possibilities.

Tie-Dyed Fabric

Tie-dyed fabric can do the work for you. It already has definable markings that can be used to your advantage. These fabrics can provide a lot of excitement and movement, and they usually have good color separation and a range of colors.

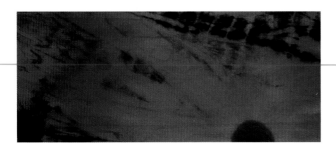

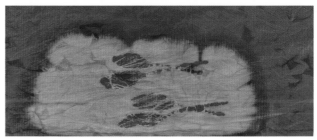

Tie-dyed fabrics are full of design potential.

Good Color-Transition Fabrics

Fabrics that have a soft color transformation work well for this process. These fabrics have a balanced change of color. The color transition is fluid, yet light enough that you can see the paints. When I look at a potential fabric, I unwind at least a yard from the bolt and hold it away from myself for better perspective. When you do this, you will probably see a hidden treasure in the fabric or get some feel for the flow and possibilities. You should never just look at it on the bolt and think you see it all. It takes at least a yard of fabric to get the proper perspective.

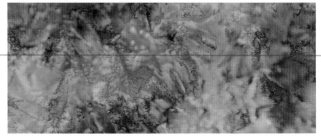

Fabrics with good color transition have a balance of color.

FINDING AND MARKING THE DESIGNS

This process is the beginning of a great quilting experience. Remember this—you are the artist, so let the design process begin. I suggest always buying more of your focus fabric than you need.

After choosing your fabric, place it on your design wall and stand back for a better perspective. Hanging your fabric on a design wall is the best way to view it and find the hidden treasures. Potential designs are much easier to see when the fabric is hanging vertically rather than lying flat on the floor or on a table. If you don't have an area large enough to stand back at least three or four feet, you can look through a camera lens or reducing glass. It's amazing how doing this will open your eyes to the things you can't see when you're close up.

Artist, take up your viewing tool, stand back, and start gazing!

What do you see? Try to find those hidden treasures using the colors of the batik for inspiration. Look for flowers or other objects such as vases, leaves, or butterflies that pop out in the fabrics. If there is a patch of green, make it a leaf, and then add flowers around the leaf. A dark circle can become a flower center, so add creative petals. You'll want to leave space for quilting in the background, so be careful not to crowd or clutter your canvas too much. Choose the area where you see the most design possibilities. This might be smack-dab in the center of the fabric. At this point you will want to identify the boundaries of the area. Use a ruler and chalk marker (I use tailor's chalk) to mark the area you want to use. Trim your fabric, leaving at least 4" to 5" beyond the chalk line on all sides.

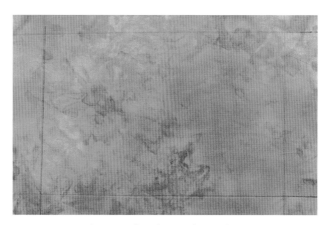

As you choose and mark your chosen design area, your creative journey begins.

Think of this as a soft guide—a guide to keep you within the chosen area yet close enough to the chalk line to add interest and achieve a balanced design. The artist always pushes the boundaries. Be free with your designs but be aware of the placement around the edges.

With the boundaries marked, you can start identifying the hidden treasures. Use a permanent marker or fabric pen in a dark color to roughly outline the found objects, making sure they're not too close together and that the design is balanced. Always using a permanent marker will ensure that the ink won't bleed or the line won't disappear before you can stitch over the outlined design. The marker you use needs to be seen over all the colors in the batik. Dark blue or deep burgundy can usually be seen on most fabrics. The markings will be covered in the thread outlining and painting process. If you're unsure of yourself, use a chalk marker to temporarily outline the designs. However, the chalk will rub off during the process, so once you're pleased with your design, trace over the chalk lines with a permanent marker before you start sewing.

I start by outlining some of the color blotches in the fabric that look like a flower, petal, or leaf shape. I then continue the design, adding more details to the flower or leaf and using my imagination to complete the design. When I have several designs or hidden treasures identified, I go back and fill in the spaces to make groupings that complement the piece as a whole.

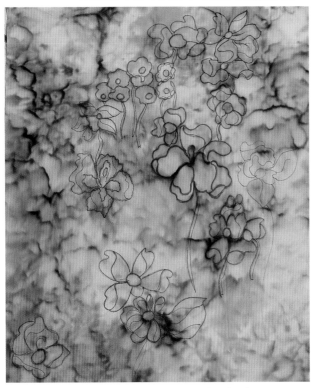

Use a permanent marker to roughly outline the shapes in the fabric that look like leaves, petals, or complete flowers.

When you're satisfied with your design, use a rotary cutter and ruler to trim the excess fabric, leaving a ¼"-wide seam allowance all around the outside of the chalk boundary line.

Evaluate Your Design

After each marking, stand back and examine your design. Outline a few shapes and then examine your design again. Continue in this manner until you're pleased with it.

If you don't have the space to stand at least a few feet away from your design wall, try looking at your marked design through a camera lens or reducing glass. The point is to look at the design with a fresh and new perspective. Viewing it from a distance helps you see objects that are not visible when you're working up close. Remember cloud gazing? How far off are those clouds anyway?

AN ARTISTIC APPROACH TO BORDERS

Through the years I have struggled with this part of the quiltmaking process. It's sad to say that I have made far too many mistakes in my effort to make perfect and balanced borders and found myself feeling disappointed in my lack of ability to balance my quilt center with perfect borders.

Then I came to the conclusion that borders were not going to challenge me anymore and decided I would focus on the quilt center. This little thought set me free. Especially when I noticed that my students were intrigued by my borders. What amazed me was that they were drawn to my basic borders. I now refer to these as KISS borders—Keep It Simple, Stitchers!

This revelation allowed me to concentrate on the quilt center and my quilting abilities. It helped me to see borders as an extension of my quilting designs rather than as a whole new element to deal with. Many artists don't border their works or even frame them. Many canvases hang on walls without a frame. Some artists leave their work unframed so as not to take away from the artistic value.

In the same way, the focus fabric and design in the quilt center generally have enough impact to stand alone without borders. So borders or no borders—it's your call. Take a look at the project photos in this book as well as the gallery photos on page 71 to help you determine if you want to add a border.

Choosing the right border fabric makes all the difference. I use a few basic yet effective border approaches.

Let the fabric do the work. Variegated or transitional fabrics go from one color to the next. Gradated fabrics stay in the same color range but transition gradually from light to dark or from dark to light. Choosing a fabric with these characteristics will add color and interest to your quilt without the need for complicated border piecing.

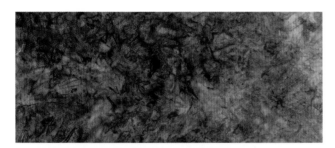

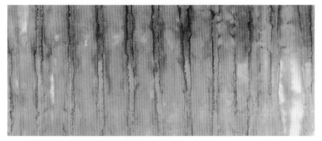

A variegated or gradated fabric can make a stunning border.

Striped, dotted, and Fairy Frost fabric (a cotton fabric with sparkles) can all set the stage for successful borders.

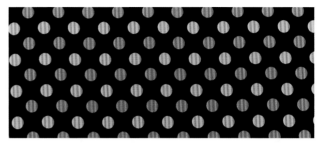

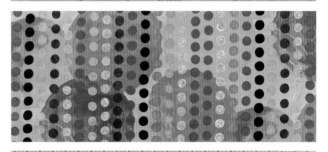

Geometrics such as dots and stripes can work well for borders, as can sparkly fabrics such as Michael Miller's Fairy Frost line.

Borders do not have to be even. They don't have to measure the same width on all four sides of your quilt, nor do they even have to be on all four sides. They don't have to be mitered or balanced. What they do need to do is complement your quilt!

IT'S ALL ABOUT THE THREAD

Thread plays an important part in the final outcome of quilts. It can actually make or break the flow and impact of the design. I use thread in my quilting as a tool to help achieve the artistic design I've envisioned. I consider thread a valuable source of color and texture. The wrong thread can overpower or downplay your design. When sizing thread it's important to remember, the smaller the number, the thicker the thread.

THREAD FOR OUTLINING THE DESIGN ELEMENTS

The first thread you'll need to select is the outline thread—the thread you'll use to outline your images.

You've already outlined your shapes with a fabric pen. Now they need to be outlined with a heavy thread. This step will help you define the area you will quilt. As we turn our quilts this way and that while machine quilting, many of us have a tendency to get lost. By outlining the designs with a dark, heavy thread, you will be able to keep your sense of direction when you go on to the next step. Heavyweight thread also comes in handy for the painting stage because it acts as a barrier to stop the paint from bleeding. See more about painting in "Painting on Fabric" on page 36.

I'm a firm believer in good-quality thread; Sulky 12-weight cotton is a favorite of mine. Dark colors work best, and I've found that chocolate brown or black thread provides a good balance for most of my work. I also recommend using solid-colored thread because variegated thread tends to get lost when the color shifts to a lighter or darker shade, depending on your fabric. When you use the heavier thread for outlining, loosen the top tension on your machine a little, usually by about one setting. For example, if your regular top tension is set at 4, you would loosen it to 3. You may need to experiment and find the setting that works best for your machine.

When you're ready to outline stitch around your marked designs, use a free-motion presser foot, a size 90/14 needle, and heavyweight thread. We'll talk about needles in "Getting Ready to Quilt" on page 22, and I'll share more about how to quilt around the designs in "Free-Motion Quilting" on page 25.

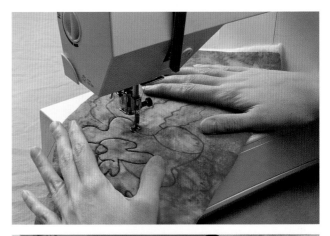

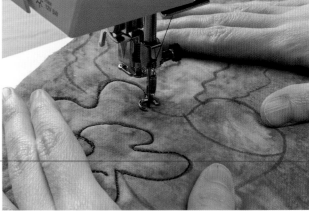

Dark, heavyweight thread defines the design area and will act as a guide for the machine quilting and painting to be done later.

THREAD FOR QUILTING THE DESIGN ELEMENTS

Equally as important as the outlining thread is the thread you choose for quilting inside the design area. Thread is available in a variety of colors, weights, and fibers. I use a variety of weights and types of thread for this process, and I change thread often. Whatever type I choose, I commonly use a 30-weight or 40-weight thread.

Your choice of thread color is more important than the weight of the thread. I use a lot of variegated rayon threads; they're excellent for shading and have a beautiful sheen. The rayon shows up on the batik fabric because of the sheen, yet it doesn't overwhelm the design. One variegated thread that adds an interesting color-wash effect is Blendables by Sulky. Be aware, however, that variegated thread can get lost in an overpowering batik. A solid-colored thread defines an area, making it stand out, and is the best thread to use where your batik is either very dark or very bright. For this part of the project, select thread colors that will guide you in the painting step. Choosing thread that enhances your design will become easier as you gain experience.

So many wonderful threads are available that can really enhance your design. It's fun to try them all.

THREAD FOR QUILTING THE BACKGROUND

For the background areas, I often choose 40-weight variegated rayon thread. It blends with the background without taking away from the main designs. When choosing the colors for this step, I suggest a variegated thread from only one color family. For instance, a soft green that goes from a light to medium to dark green is often more effective than a variegated thread that goes from one color to another. Multicolored thread can overpower your design area and muddy or confuse your quilt. Solid-colored thread can also be a good choice if it doesn't overpower your batik fabric and the design area. Soft and understated thread will enhance your artistic design area, drawing the viewer's eyes to your design rather than to the background.

Variegated thread in the same color family gives a more understated look than one that jumps from one color to another.

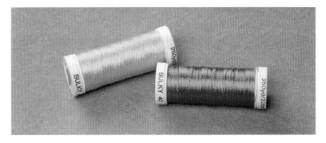

Choose solid-colored threads that don't overwhelm your artistic design.

Choosing the Correct Thread

Here's a summary of my recommendations for the different threads used in the process.

Outlining the Design Elements: Use heavy-weight thread in a dark, solid color such as chocolate brown or black; Sulky 12-weight cotton is a good choice.

Quilting the Design Elements: Use 30-weight or 40-weight thread in the color of your choice. Solid colors work best for batiks that are very dark or very bright; variegated threads are fine with other batiks.

Quilting the Background: Use 40-weight rayon thread in variegated or solid colors that blend with the background.

THREAD FOR THE BOBBIN

When teaching, I'm often asked about bobbin thread. There is much to say about bobbins, but telling you what to do and working out the kinks are two different things. I almost cringe when students are having problems with their bobbins. The thread doesn't hold all the answers, nor does the bobbin case; they go hand in hand and need to be addressed together.

I strive to have the backs of my quilts showcase my artistry as much as the quilt fronts. It delights me to hear people say the back is just as beautiful as the front. Making it happen is the challenge.

Knots of thread on the back are oh so pesky, and when the top thread shows through—ugh. So what's a quilter to do? Here are a few pointers.

- As I move from one design area to another on the same quilt, I change my bobbin thread often.

- If you use the same thread in the bobbin as in the top, many problems vanish. If the top thread does show on the back of the quilt, it's not noticeable because they're the same color.

- In some of my quilts, I've used a very fine bobbin-weight thread in the bobbin. I loosen my top tension a bit so the top thread will show through on the back. This looks beautiful and it's so easy to do. The machine takes care of the artistic-looking back if you take care of the top. The top thread just barely comes to the back, creating a spectacular look.

- Always test your thread on the exact fabric combination used for your quilt—use scraps of your top fabric, batting, and backing fabric. If you use different fabrics, you will not get true test results.

Try This with Your Bobbin

Use a 40-weight cotton thread in the bobbin for quilting inside the design area and a bobbin-weight thread in the bobbin for the background quilting. I have found this very effective.

The back of a quilt can look just as gorgeous as the
front when you use the right thread combination.

QUILTING YOUR ART QUILT

I believe and teach that before you can quilt a top successfully, you need all the tools. Throughout my years of quilting and teaching, I have discovered that when you have the tools, the artistic elements and design concepts come more naturally. You can then concentrate on the actual quilting. I always share this information with my students before we even touch a sewing machine.

GETTING READY TO QUILT

Needles are important. Did you know that a needle designed specifically for machine quilting really does have something unique to offer? I can tell if I'm using a machine quilting needle by the way my quilt top moves as I'm quilting. The quilting needle has a more tapered end and is longer than other sewing machine needles; this allows the needle to glide with ease through the three layers. The size of the needle you use depends on the thread; the smaller the number, the finer the needle. For instance, an 80/12 needle is smaller than a 90/14 needle. For very thick thread such as a 12-weight, I use a 90/14 needle. The eye and shaft are larger, which makes the thread go through the needle easier. On the other hand, a needle that's too large for the thread size causes slack in the thread as it goes through the needle, which can cause jumps in the thread or skipped stitches. If I'm using a 30-weight or 40-weight thread, I use an 80/12 quilting needle, which is the needle size I used in all the projects in this book.

Thread for Art Quilts

Thread is an important part in the process as well. For detailed information regarding different threads and how to select the correct thread for each step, turn to "It's All about the Thread" on page 18.

The single-hole or straight-stitch needle plate is one tool I wouldn't want to be without. The small needle hole confines the needle to one spot and provides fabric support all around the needle. When you use a wide-slot needle plate, the needle can travel in that slot as you turn corners and move your quilt. This can hinder your movement and cause puckers and tucks in the fabric. The single-hole needle plate is your friend; it gently guides the needle straight down into the fabric. You will notice a big difference with this plate.

Machingers gloves are a favorite for my students. They are lightweight and breathable, and they have rubber tips that help you grip the quilt as you move it under the needle. **The Quilt Sew Easy hoop** by Heavenly Notion is a horseshoe-shaped piece of flexible plastic with foam cushions underneath that grab your fabrics, helping you move them while resting your hands on the raised handles. Maneuvering the quilt can be a source of aggravation if you don't have the proper tools and know-how. These are two of the many products available to help with this.

The SewSlip silcone sheet is one of the best tools to hit the market for quilters today. It has a hole in the center that fits over the needle plate on your sewing machine. Its slick surface eliminates drag on your quilt and helps your stitch quality. Now I couldn't imagine being without one, and I wonder how I managed in the past. Most extender tables have a plastic top with a resistant surface that makes it difficult to move your quilt, but the teflon sheet supplies a pleasurable, smooth surface for quilts to glide over.

A proper work space is important. Ergonomics play a role in the overall quilting, believe it or not. If you're sitting at the wrong height or having trouble with your quilt top falling off your table or getting caught on things, your quilting will be affected. If your shoulders

and wrists ache, your movements may become jerky and your stitches irregular. All of these things add unnecessary stress to you and your body, but the problems can be rectified. By changing a few habits and a few things in your sewing room or area, you can eliminate stress and end up with better quality quilting. Here are a few inexpensive remedies to help you wherever your sewing area may be.

- If you have a sewing-machine cabinet with the quilter's extension on the back, this is an ideal work surface. If your sewing machine sits on top of a table or drops down into a cabinet without the extended surface on the back, push your table or cabinet up against the wall so that you're facing the wall as you

sew. The wall will prevent your quilt from falling off the edge of the table. This is important, because the quilt becomes heavy and can cause broken needles, uneven stitches, and stress on arms and shoulders.

- If your machine sits on top of a table, your quilts are probably getting hung up on the edges of the extended sewing table or on the sewing machine. It helps a great deal to pile heavy books around your machine to build up an even surface area to support your quilt. I have all the proper equipment in my studio. However, when I'm quilting on a large quilt, I need to support the quilt on my left side. To do this, I move my ironing board close to my machine and cover it with a smooth, slick plastic tablecloth so that my quilt can move easily. Spreading the quilt out over a larger area relieves a lot of the bulkiness and is a big help. When you aren't fighting the movement of the quilt, you can concentrate on the quilting design.

- Something else I practice and tell my students to practice is to take breaks frequently, at least every half hour. Your body, mind, and eyes need the rest. When you come back, you'll be surprised how refreshed you'll feel, and you'll be ready to design again.

Proper Quilting Position

As you're sitting at your table where you'll be quilting, push yourself away from that area and put your forearms out in front of you at waist level. *How do they feel?* Raise them up where you usually quilt. *Hmmm . . . how do they feel now?* You probably felt uncomfortable; maybe you felt it in your shoulders or the back of your neck. Many of us are in this position when quilting. If you raise your chair, sit on a cushion, or do whatever it takes to keep your arms at waist level, you will have much more control over your work and be more comfortable.

READY, SET, SANDWICH

This is my favorite topic to teach beginners and those who have struggled with the process of sandwiching or basting a quilt. Sometimes ignorance is bliss. In this case, it was for me. Since I taught myself to quilt, I didn't know there were rules to follow. I grew up loving to iron, so to iron my batting was only natural. Below, I share my method with you.

PRESSING

The first thing that makes a quilt flat is the pressing process. I press all seam allowances open, which gives the top a flatter surface with fewer bumps to quilt over, especially where seams meet in the same area. I prefer to press as I go, laying my quilt top face down on top of 100%-cotton batting. I like to double the batting to give it even more loft for pressing. Then, I press the

Choose a Good Batting

I'm a firm believer in good batting. In fact, I'm a batting snob. In my experience, Fairfield Soft Touch is outstanding for several reasons. It's as soft as the label states, it holds its shape, and it's like quilting through butter. The light weight also makes it easy to move. I know you may have your favorite batting, but if you have never tried this batting, try it just once. You may fall in love with it as so many of us have. In my area the shops can hardly keep it in stock.

seam allowances open over the batting. This process allows the fabric to sink down into the batting loft, which gently spreads the fabric properly so that as you quilt your top, there's less shifting. I refer to this as the proper press. You will actually see the seam lines on the batting. When my complete top is finished, I repeat this process once more. It's not as tedious as it sounds, and it eliminates a multitude of problems later. I use steam but I don't scrub the iron back and forth. I start at the top of the quilt and lightly press as I work toward the bottom.

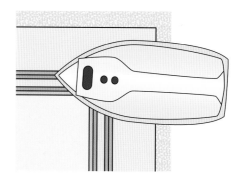

I recommend that you cut the backing at least 3" larger than the quilt top on all sides. For quilts wider than the width of your backing fabric, you'll need to piece the backing. When piecing the backing, be sure to trim off the selvages before sewing the pieces together. After stitching, I place my backing on top of my double layer of batting. Then I steam press the backing, going from top to bottom in one direction and pressing any seam allowances open to reduce bulk.

Batting that's just out of the package is wrinkled. If you smooth it out by hand, there is a strong possibility that the batting will pucker and fold, which causes problems in the quilting process. I steam press my 100%-cotton batting in the same manner as I do the backing and top. Don't try this with fusible batting, blends, or polyester batting. Polyester batting will melt unless you hold the iron high enough above the batting so that you're not touching it.

BASTING

Spread the prepared backing wrong side up on a flat, clean surface. Center the pressed batting over the backing and steam press the two together. Then center the prepared top right side up over the batting and steam press the three layers together. If you're using Soft Touch batting and a few other 100%-cotton battings, you will notice that the three layers stick together without any basting spray glues.

This process will help eliminate puckers, top movement, and lumps and bumps, and you will not have to closely pin baste the layers together. I place pins 12" to 20" apart, depending on the quilt top, to ensure a larger quilting area without having to deal with troublesome pins.

Warning about Three-Layer Steaming

Just to warn you—when you use steam, it stays in the three layers for a short time. If you turn the backing over and it has ripples, don't worry, it's just the steam. It will return to normal after the steam has dissipated.

Has this ever happened to you? I struggled with this in several of my quilts. My quilt top would end up longer than the backing and batting. I couldn't for the life of me figure out how it happened. I measured again and again, I cut my backing and batting a little larger all around, and still I had more quilt top than backing and batting. *What happened?* How could I make sure it never happened again?

There are a few reasons this happens. One problem may be your pressing. But consider this: many of our quilts are made from various fabrics and many pieces. Some pieces have bias edges. As you quilt, they naturally spread out, or in other words, they grow. But your batting and backing are not usually made of many pieces, and they don't grow. So if you start quilting on one side or at the top of the quilt and work in one direction, you may be causing your quilt top to grow without realizing it. By starting in the center of the quilt and working toward the outside edges, your quilt will grow in all four directions equally.

FREE-MOTION QUILTING

You'll begin by making a few necessary adjustments to your sewing machine. Free-motion quilting requires feed dogs to be dropped. For machines that do not have that function, you may have a plastic cover.

Personal Motor Speed

Finding your personal motor speed is important, because we all go through life differently. Here is my theory on personal motor speed. Most would categorize me as hyper. Let's just say that I often hear comments like, "Do you ever sleep or slow down?" Translated, that means I need to quilt at a fast pace. If I were to put my speed on slow, I would be frustrated, probably break needles, and have a very ugly stitch and no control. On the other hand, if you tend to be mellow and carefree, then you will need to quilt in the same manner. So my theory is, what's true of your personality, will also be true of your personal motor speed. This does not mean you need to speed through everything. It means go the speed that suits you so that you can maintain an even speed. I don't put my pedal to the metal, but my motor speed is high, so I have that option. Aim for an even, steady speed, where the hands and foot are moving at pretty much an equal pace.

Or you can cover them with a piece of cardboard. If your machine has a needle-stop down setting (so the needle stops in the down position), use it. This tremendous tool holds your fabric in place as you go around corners and makes pausing easier too. Loosen the presser-foot tension on the right side or top of your machine to lighten the pressure on the fabric (your machine may not have this option). If you haven't already done so, change to the single-hole needle plate.

For more information on machine quilting, refer to one of the many available machine-quilting books, such as *Machine Quilting Made Easy!* (Martingale & Company, 2003).

Loosen the presser-foot tension.

Use an open-toe free-motion foot or darning foot. Change the needle to one that is the correct size for the thread you're using and loosen the top tension, if applicable.

To begin free-motion quilting, hold the fabric with your hands at the sides of the needle and begin stitching. Start in the center of the area you're quilting and work outward toward the edges. Quilt all the marked design lines using a dark-colored 12-weight thread. Then, using a rayon variegated or solid-colored thread, quilt inside all the areas within the outline-stitched designs.

During this process you will have to cut and change your thread often to move to the next design area. Press after each move to avoid puckering and other difficulties later. Clip all loose threads before you go on to the next design. That way, when this task is completed, it really is completed; you won't have to go back and stress over all those tangled loose ends.

Last, quilt all the background areas around the outlined designs, including any feather designs.

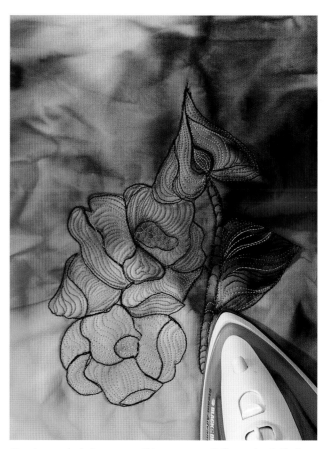

Pressing each design area will keep your quilt flat and wrinkle free.

Artistic No-Mark Quilting

Marks are hard to follow for some of us, but if you develop a few designs, you can turn them into many quilting designs. If you're a doodler, you already have a head start; you can turn your doodles into quilting designs. Doodle when you have downtime so that the doodles become ingrained in your mind and get to be automatic. Doodling actually trains your hand and eye and becomes natural after a while. The more you practice on paper, the more you're likely to get positive results on your quilt top. You can do this with your own artistic sense of design.

QUILTING DESIGNS FOR ART QUILTS

In this section I've compiled several basic stitches. You can practice each line by using paper and pencil before stitching it on your quilt. The one-stroke samples can lead to many design possibilities. I encourage you to play with them and design your own quilting patterns. I've also included a progression showing how to combine the basic stitches with filler stitches. I hope this helps you gain a greater understanding and allows you to see more possibilities for creating your own designs.

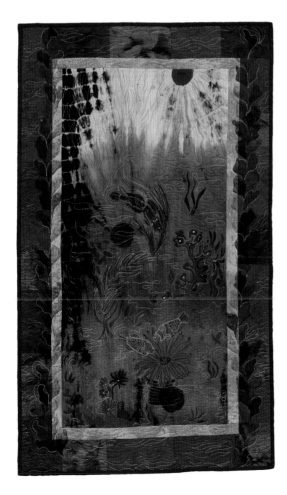

BASIC CURVES

One basic stroke can turn into a beautifully quilted project. This small curve has a wealth of possibilities.

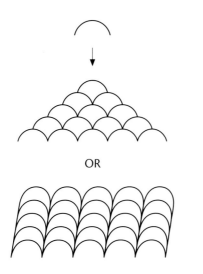

OR

Draw a slightly curvy line with the shape going one direction in the first row and then reversing the direction in the next row, following the curve as shown.

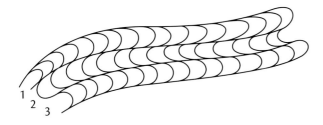

Draw two curvy lines that begin parallel and then spread apart at one end. Then go back and add a pattern inside the lines.

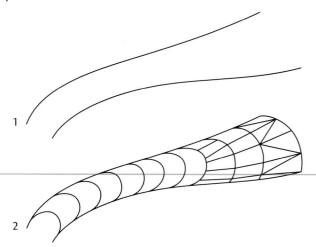

Again draw two curvy lines that begin parallel and then spread apart at one end. Where the lines spread apart, try another pattern inside the lines.

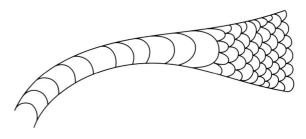

FEATHER DESIGN

The feather quilting design is beloved by most quilters, but many are intimidated by it. To take the mystery out of this beautiful design, start by using chalk to mark a curvy line. Start sewing at the base of the chalk line, and follow the direction of the arrows as shown. Relax and practice this stunning design.

The next design is similar to a feather design in that it travels and is continuous. I call it a traveling flower, and it's great for borders. This is an easy design that can go in many different directions.

Start →

FILLER STITCHES

Filler stitches can be used to fill the background area with quilting.

The W stitch is an easy design that can be done in various sizes.

Circles or small clusters take a little patience; the secret is to go over the same lines to complete the circle and advance to the next circle.

Connecting balls look best if they're different sizes. Make the designs inside the balls go in different directions to add movement.

Traveling loops can go in any direction to fill areas that are hard to reach or need a lot of filling with little effort.

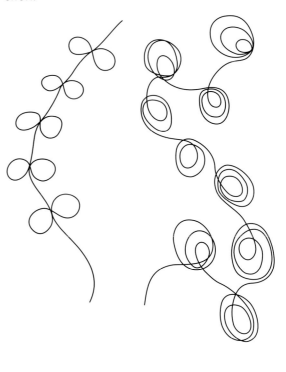

QUILTING INSIDE FLOWERS AND LEAVES

Directional quilting inside design areas will help you determine your paint colors and decide how to use paint for shading and highlighting the designs.

Flowers. Use quilting lines to define the flower shape and create petals. Notice how the same basic shape can be quilted in several ways to achieve different results.

Leaves. Quilting lines define the leaf shape and give the impression that the leaf is dimensional.

Flower and leaf. Change the direction of the quilting lines to delineate the shapes.

CONNECTING THE DESIGNS

After quilting inside all the flowers and leaves, add stems to connect them to each other.

Next, add feather quilting designs to the open area in the background.

Finally, outline quilt around the flower and leaf designs.
Then use the designs in "Basic Curves" and "Filler
Stitches" to fill in the background quilting.

FINISHING YOUR ART QUILT

The following information will help give your art quilt the perfect finishing touch.

BORDERS MADE PERFECT

Wavy borders have been a problem since the beginning of time. I have my own remedy that works like a charm every time. I cut the outer border wider than the desired final width and make the batting and backing that much larger as well. During the quilting process, quilters grab the edges of the quilt, which causes the edges to become distorted. Making the borders wider than the finished size of the quilt allows us to trim the borders to the intended size and cut off the distorted, wavy edge. I quilt all the way to the outer edge. When I'm finished with all the quilting, I trim the excess border along with the excess batting and backing. With this method, your borders will be perfectly straight—a quilter's dream.

To square up your quilt, align the desired border width on the ruler with the seam line of the outer border. For example, if you want the finished width of the outer border to be 3" wide, you would align the 3¼" line on the ruler with the seam line (the finished border width of 3" plus ¼"-wide seam allowance). Using a rotary cutter, cut along the edge of the ruler and trim the outer border to the width specified in the project instructions. Trim the excess border, batting, and backing from all four sides. Use a square ruler to square up each corner.

ADDING A HANGING SLEEVE

If you plan to hang your finished quilt, sew a hanging sleeve to the upper back now, before you bind the quilt.

Cut a 9"-wide strip of fabric equal to the width of your quilt. On each short end of the strip, fold over ½",

Square up the quilt.

and then fold ½" again to make a hem. Press and stitch by machine.

Fold the strip in half lengthwise, with wrong sides together, and baste the raw edges to the upper edge of the back of your quilt. These raw edges will be secured when you sew on the binding. Your quilt should be about 1" wider than the sleeve on both sides.

When you pin the bottom of the sleeve to the back, roll the edge up ¼". This adds a little extra space for the hanging rod. Slip-stitch the ends and bottom edge of the sleeve to the backing fabric. Stitching down the ends keeps the rod from being inserted next to the quilt backing.

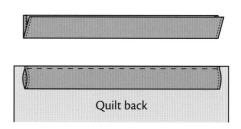

Quilt back

BINDING YOUR QUILT

The projects in this book include yardage for double-fold binding that is cut 2½" wide.

1. Cut binding strips as instructed for the project you're making, cutting across the width of the fabric. Overlap the ends of the strips, with right sides together, as shown. Sew diagonally from corner to corner, trim off the outside corner, leaving a ¼"-wide seam allowance, and press the seam allowance open.

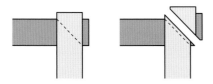

2. When all the strips have been stitched together and pressed, cut one end at a 45° angle. Press the binding in half lengthwise, wrong sides together, aligning the raw edges.

Fold line

3. Beginning with the angled end of the strip, place the binding along one side of the quilt (not at a corner) and align the raw edge of the strip with the raw edge of the quilt top. Leaving the first 8" unstitched, stitch the binding to the quilt using a ¼"-wide seam allowance and the edge of the quilt as a guide. At the first corner, stop sewing ¼" from the quilt edge and backstitch. Clip the thread and remove the quilt from the machine.

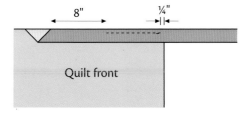

8"   ¼"

Quilt front

4. Rotate the quilt 90° so that you're ready to sew down the next side. Fold the binding strip up so that the edge of the binding is even with the edge of the quilt. Then fold it down again to miter the corners, keeping the fold even with the edge of the quilt. Begin with a backstitch at the fold of the binding

and continue stitching along the edge of the quilt top, mitering each corner as you come to it.

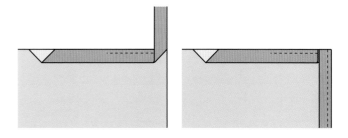

5. Stop sewing when you're about 10" from where you began. Clip the thread and remove your quilt from the machine. Lay the beginning tail flat on the quilt top. Overlap the end of the binding over the beginning. Trim the ends so that the overlap measures 2½". Sew the two ends together as shown and trim, leaving a ¼"-wide seam allowance. Press the seam allowance; then refold the binding in half and press the fold. Lay the binding flat along the quilt edge and stitch in place.

Overlap of ends

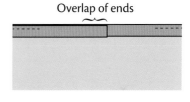

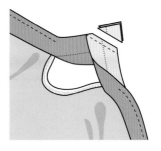

6. Fold the edge of the binding to the back of the quilt and pin in place so that the folded edge covers the row of machine stitching. Using thread that matches your binding, hand stitch the binding in place, mitering each corner.

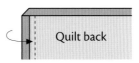

Quilt back

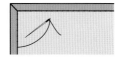

PAINTING ON FABRIC

Welcome to the artistic world of adding paint to your project. This is a leap of faith for some of us, but let me reassure you, it can be addictive. If you were ever intimidated or fearful of taking paintbrush in hand and actually turning your quilt into art—don't be. You already have completed most of the project and have laid a foundation for the next step. Relax and prepare yourself for a journey into the art-quilt world.

WHAT PAINTS TO USE

I use a variety of products to obtain the colors I want, and I'd like to share a few of them with you. First you need to determine if the paint is made for fabric and won't bleed. Even when the product says it's made for fabric, I test it first to make sure. I want my paint to be soft and pliable and to maintain the natural softness of the fabric. I often combine paints to make my own colors, and most of the time I water them down so they will glide on better.

Tsukineko All-Purpose Ink (pronounced SUEKINECHO) is a dream to use. It's washable, permanent when heat set, nontoxic, and acid free. It comes in 36 colors and is best used with Fantastix paint sticks. The ink is adaptable to other paints, and it blends, mixes, and waters down easily for a watercolor effect. The ink can also be used to dye your own fabrics. Fantastix paint sticks are soft, uninked, reusable applicators that are available in your choice of two tips—pointed brush tip or rounded bullet tip. Dipping just the tip into the ink fills the fibers and holds the ink in for quite a long time. Be sure to get the cover for the tips when you purchase them so the ink will stay on the tip while in storage. The applicator can be washed in warm soapy water to reuse with a different color. The paint sticks give you better support than a regular brush, especially when you're going for the watercolor look.

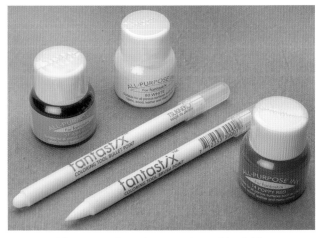

All-purpose inks and paint sticks are blendable, washable, and versatile.

Fabrico markers by Tsukineko are also washable, acid free, nontoxic, and permanent when heat set. They're available in 36 colors, and each marker has a dual tip—bullet and brush. The markers are great for shading and outlining, bringing to life your other paints and inks that don't have enough color or contrast.

Markers are easy to use and specifically designed for smooth ink flow.

VersaCraft ink pads by Tsukineko are washable, acid free, nontoxic, permanent when heat set, and fun. They come in 36 colors and two 12-color pads. They're used for stamping and stenciling and are color coordinated with the Fabrico markers. You can use them just like paint. Glide a brush across the ink pad and dip it slightly in water. You can also use a stamp or sponge dauber.

Multicolored pads offer a convenient variety of colors.

Jacquard has three products that I use in my work. All the products are nontoxic, water-based, and permanent when heat set. They can be watered down and mixed with inks. With most of these products, I use a paintbrush with a small brush point.

• Dye-na-Flow is an actual dye. When you're dying a fabric, it's always necessary to prewash it to remove the sizing so that the dye can be absorbed into the fabric. After prewashing the fabric, apply Dye-na-Flow with a brush, cloth, or dropper, and then sprinkle it with water and watch it spread. When you're satisfied with the results, let it set for 24 hours. Heat set the fabric using a dry iron at the correct temperature setting for the fabric, and it's ready to use. Dye-na-Flow can also be used as paint.

• Textile Traditional is a little thicker paint with more intense color. I water this product down because it's thicker than I want. Undiluted, it lies on the surface of the fabric, and when dry, it has a hard feel to it. When watered down, the paint doesn't do that.

• Lumiere is beautiful and comes in gorgeous colors that have a gold, silver, or bronze mix in them. They stand out and are exquisite. I water them down quite a bit. The more water you add, the more gold, silver, or bronze comes out of the brush. The paints are thick, and if not watered down they will give a heavy and overpowering look to the fabric.

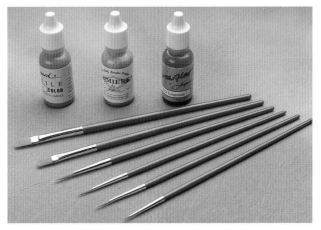

All three types of paint work together well to produce stunning quilts.

Now you have your artist pallet of beautiful products; notice that all of them are nontoxic—the only way to go.

Save Those Bottle Caps

We all have bottle caps around the house. Save all your caps from water bottles, milk jugs, or what have you. They come in handy for small amounts of paint and for mixing colors.

An assortment of saved bottle caps can be collected easily.

Even if you don't realize it yet, chances are you have a sense of art inside you just waiting to be discovered. Are you a gardener who finds peace and joy in the beautiful plants and flowers you've chosen and carefully placed? Do you enjoy decorating your home with just the right furniture, art, drapes, pillows, and accessories? Perhaps you have an eye for jewelry, fashion, and makeup. All of these are creative pursuits and you, my friend, are an artist.

QUILTING MAKES WAY FOR PAINTING

By first stitching around the hidden treasures in your fabric, you have already started the process of letting your quilting prepare the way for painting your creation. The quilting inside the outlined designs will help you determine the colors of the paints you want to use. The direction of the quilting lines inside the petals and leaves will help you use paints for shading and highlighting. If you quilted feathers, you will already have an area where you can add paint.

PAINTING YOUR ART QUILT

For some of us, this process can be overwhelming. Your first thought might be, "Where do I start?" I will guide you through the steps; it's actually not as difficult or intimidating as it may look. In my classes, I find that some students have reservations about this process. Yet once they start, they soar right through it with great zeal and confidence. Here are a few tips to help you get started. Enjoy the process as you find the hidden artist inside.

To start, prepare your work space. Use plastic tablecloths to cover the work surface. Have old towels handy to wipe paintbrushes on. You'll need a cup or small bowl to place paintbrushes in, and you'll need a spray bottle or dropper to add water to the paint, if needed. If you do accidentally spill or splatter something, you can usually clean it up right away with soap and cold water. If all else fails, a cleaning product such as OxiClean works wonders on most stains.

The inside of your design should already be quilted. You'll be painting inside the dark outline-stitched lines, but don't worry about painting over the quilting lines. The quilting will give you an idea of what color family to use for your flower or leaf and will lead you to the first step—choosing the right color.

Choosing the right color depends on the type of ink, fabric pen, or paint you have chosen. I highly suggest purchasing a combination of inks, fabric pens, and paints. I use all three, layering them in most of my work to achieve the desired dimension and color.

Let's walk through this process.

1. Choose the color you plan to use. Let's say you're painting your first flower in red. A red flower is made up of many shades of red, from dark to light. So if you're  using All Purpose Ink, start by dipping the Fantastix stick into a light shade of red. Lightly brush over your flower petal, leaving just a hint of red. The ink will fade a little when it's dry, and it should take only a few minutes to dry.

2. After the ink is dry, you will know if the petal needs a little more color. If needed, add a little more ink. If not, go on to the next step.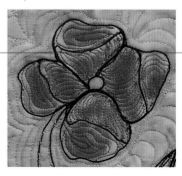

3. Next you'll be *shading* the petal. I usually use ink for this step and repeat it as many times as needed to achieve the desired effect. Use a burgundy or darker shade of red

and go over the areas near the center of the petal to add a darker color. I also shade the outside edges with the darker ink and blend the colors toward the center.

4. Now we'll use the paints. To bring your flower to life, use any combination of paints you want. As mentioned earlier, I water down most of my paints to help them

disappear into the fabrics. I do this by using a spray bottle or dropper. Put a small amount of the paint color you want to use into a bottle cap or whatever you're using to mix your paints. Use the spray bottle or dropper to add a tiny amount of water to thin the paint. Apply the paint color to the center of each petal, not going over too far and covering up the darker shading, but blending. I usually use the Textile Traditions and Lumiere paints at this point. It's a good idea to frequently stand back to get the full effect of what is needed.

5. After you're satisfied with the outcome of step 4, use the fabric pens to draw in the details of the stems, the pistils, or even the edges of the petals to define

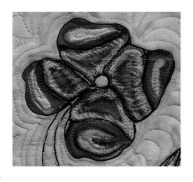

them. For this step you can use either a darker color in the same color family, or a black or dark brown pen to add depth.

6. I love to add dots to many of my quilts. They add visual interest and keep the eye moving around the quilt. I use white ink for this step and a very thin, fine fabric

brush. Dip the brush tip into the ink and paint dots on your quilt. The paint dries almost immediately, so smearing usually isn't a problem.

Painting Tip

If you've gone over the same flower too much or your flower just doesn't show up or it's too dark, you can change this by adding white textile paint or white ink over the surface area you don't like. Wait for the paint to dry and repaint the problem area. White also adds highlights, so if you want an area to stand out more, add dabs of white.

I also paint inside the quilted feather designs. The process is the same, just less involved. You can use a fabric pen, ink, or paint. You might want to combine all three to achieve the desired results. Just paint inside the stitched lines, let dry, and then heat set. You may even want to add a few dots as I did in "Dot, Dot, Dot Wall Art" on page 54.

Paint inside the feather designs.

EMBELLISHMENTS

Embellishments could fill another book, so for the projects in this book, I've selected a few of my favorites. One thing to keep in mind when considering embellishments is the focus, or focal point, of the project you are making. You have already quilted and painted your project. The embellishments should enhance or complement your design, not overwhelm it. For that reason, I've narrowed the techniques down to just a few. Embellishing is always done after the project is completed and is the icing on the cake. Make it your own.

CRYSTALS

I love hot-fix crystals. They add glitter and glitz to the surface of the project. On flower petals the tiny 2 mm crystals can look like dew. The solid black crystals look like seeds in the middle of flowers. Best of all, the crystals are easy to apply to your quilt.

You'll need an applicator wand for your hot-fix crystals, which have a heat-activated glue applied to the back. The applicator comes with tips in several sizes to match the size of the crystal. To apply the crystals, it's important to have the correct-size tip on the applicator. Follow the manufacturer's instructions. Pick up each crystal with the heating wand and let the crystal set for a few seconds so the glue can get hot enough to soften and stick to your project. Then apply the crystal directly to your project. When applied properly, crystals are very secure.

Crystals are available in a rainbow of colors and sizes. You'll need an applicator wand and various tips to apply heat-set crystals.

BEADS

Beading by hand can add sparkle and pizzazz to your project. There are many types, colors, and sizes of beads. Your project will define the size and shape of beads you choose. When it comes to adding beads, it's good to remember that if you want them to show, they'll need to contrast with the area in which you plan to stitch them.

Seed beads are small and mostly used as filler beads. They can be added to the end of the pistils in the flower center or clustered around the edges of your flower to give a ruffled effect. When using seed beads or any of the beads with small holes, you will need a beading needle. A beading needle is a long, thin needle that is very sharp and will easily go through the top two layers of the quilt.

Choose colors and bead styles that will complement your project.

Thread for beading has brought up a lot of questions. The thread I use depends on my project. Many beads are transparent, and most beaders prefer a thread color that matches the color of the beads. However, some beaders choose a thread color to match the color of their fabric or project. This is your decision and may change with each project. On cotton fabric, I use a regular 50-weight cotton thread. On silk or a delicate fabric, use a fine silk thread (60- to 100-weight).

Nymo beading thread is a strong nylon thread that is commonly used by beaders. However, it can be stiff and tangle easily. To compensate, use beeswax, Thread Heaven thread conditioner, or a dryer sheet (which works amazingly well) to help keep your thread from becoming tangled.

If you've never beaded, there are many good beginner books on beading that you can refer to for detailed instructions. To begin, cut a piece of thread about 20" long. Thread your needle, double the thread, and tie a tiny knot in the end. You're ready to bead. Insert the needle in the top layer, about where you want to place the bead, and sew through the top two layers only (the quilt top and batting). Pull the needle out at the point where you want to place a bead and gently pull the thread until the knot pops through the fabric and into the batting.

Pick up a bead with the needle and push it down the thread to the fabric. Insert the needle into the two layers close to the bead. Slide the needle under the bead (through the two layers), coming back up again close to where you began. Insert the needle through the bead and then into the quilt layers to secure the bead. Repeat to sew on the next bead. Be aware of the placement of the next bead. If the distance between beads is more than $\frac{1}{8}$", I suggest knotting and cutting the thread after each bead. You don't want the thread between beads to be too long because it can stretch and lose strength over a distance.

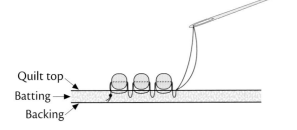

Quilt top
Batting
Backing

To sew a cluster of seed beads, begin as before, and then pick up five beads with the needle and push them down to the fabric. Before inserting the needle again into the two layers, make sure to allow enough space so the beads will lie flat. To secure the beads to the quilt,

insert the needle in the center bead and take a stitch in the same manner as you did for a single bead.

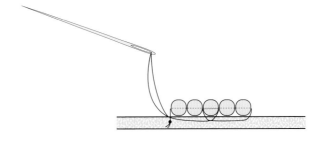

To end a section of beading, wrap the thread around the needle three or four times and insert the needle into the top two layers. (This will make a knot that will be embedded in the batting.) Pull the needle out and gently pull the thread until the knot pops through the fabric and into the batting; cut the thread at the quilt's surface.

Bugle beads are long, cylindrical beads that add a lot of shine to the quilt surface. They can be difficult to work with because of the way they're made. The beads have rough edges that can cut the thread, usually long after the project is completed. To prevent this, add a seed bead to each end of the bugle bead before inserting the needle back into the fabric.

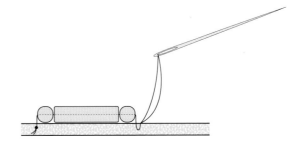

MICRO BEADS

Micro beads add dimension along with a flavor of realism. These tiny 1 mm beads have no holes and must be glued in place with good fabric glue. I apply the glue to the area I want to embellish and then pour an abundance of beads onto the area, manipulating them into a heap or pile on top of the glue. I go back often while the glue is drying and press the tiny beads into the glue. When the glue is dry, I shake the excess beads into a larger plastic bag to reuse them. A lot of these tiny beads will fall off during the process, and you may have to add more glue on top of the already-glued beads to fill in empty spaces. Once they're on and dried, the beads will hold up very well.

Micro beads add sparkle, color, and texture to your project.

FABRIC-COVERED BUTTONS

Covered buttons are a wonderful embellishment. They can be purchased in kits, come in a large range of sizes, and allow you to choose fabric to match the project. Many times, instead of sewing them on the project, I cut off the shank and *glue* the buttons to my fabric. They make interesting flower centers. Instructions for making covered buttons come with the kits and are easy to follow.

Fabric-covered buttons add variety to your embellishments.

YO-YOS

Yo-yos are another quick, inexpensive, and fun embellishment. The yo-yos of today are not the same ones our grandmothers made. We have such beautiful fabrics to choose from. Try silk, velvet, satin, sparkle fabrics, or some of the batiks you're using in your project. Make yo-yos in different sizes and colors; then embellish them with crystals or beads.

Vary the fabrics, sizes, and colors of your yo-yo embellishments to create a distinctive look.

To make a yo-yo, cut a circle 1" larger than your desired size. Thread a needle with matching thread and knot the ends together. Finger-press under the edges of the circle about $\frac{1}{8}$". Sew a running stitch close to the folded edge of the circle. When you have stitched completely around the circle, pull up the thread tightly to gather the circle edge; knot the end of the threads to secure them. You'll have a perfect yo-yo.

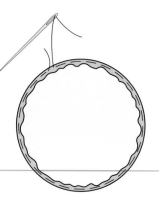

THE PROJECTS

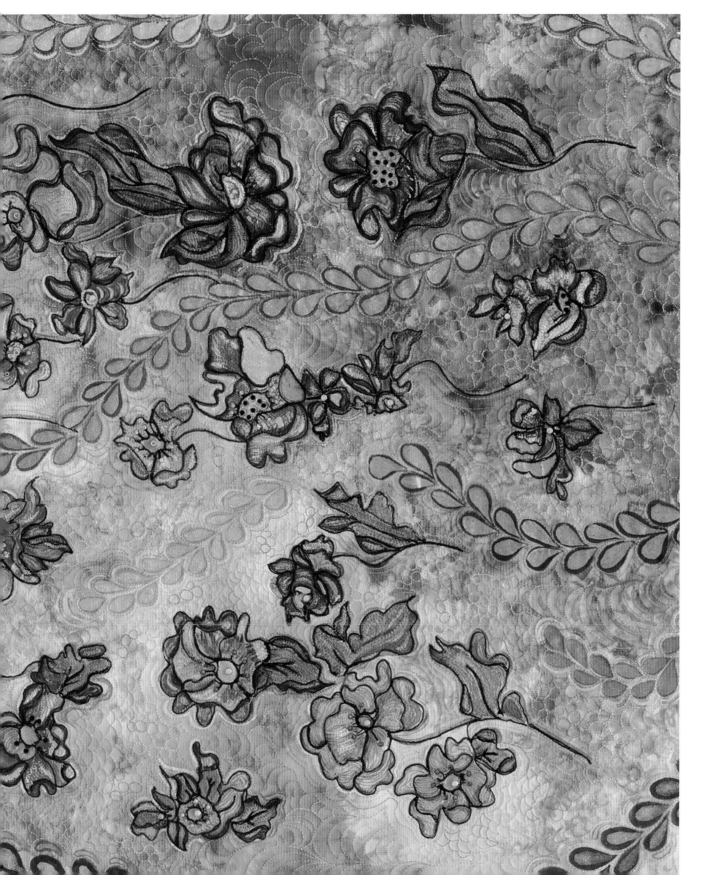

LA PETITE FLORAL
WALL QUILT

This small-scale project is
designed to help you become
comfortable with the techniques. I know you'll find it
less intimidating than you antici-
pated. Just remember to relax, use your
imagination, and create as you see it through your
artistic eye. You are about to experience joy and freedom as you hunt for the hidden treasures in your
carefully and thoughtfully chosen batik or hand-dyed
fabric. Remember, stand back, capture the movement
and design in the fabric, relax, and have fun.

Finished size: 28½" x 42½"

MATERIALS

Yardage is based on 42"-wide fabric.

1 yard of light small-scale batik or hand-dyed
   fabric for quilt center

1 yard of fabric for outer border and binding

¼ yard of fabric for inner border

1½ yards of dark solid fabric for backing

36" x 50" piece of batting

12-weight dark cotton thread for outlining flowers

40-weight rayon or cotton variegated thread to
   match and enhance flowers

40-weight white rayon thread for bobbin

Fabric paints

Hot-fix crystals, buttons, beads, and other
   embellishments

Chalk marker

Permanent marker

CUTTING

From the batik or hand-dyed fabric, cut:
1 piece, 25" x 42"

From the inner-border fabric, cut:
4 strips, 1½" x 42"

From the outer-border fabric, cut:
4 strips, 4½" x 42"

4 strips, 2½" x 42"

Designed and quilted by Judi
Dains

ARTISTIC DESIGN SELECTION

1. Place the batik or hand-dyed quilt center on your design wall. Referring to "Finding and Marking the Designs" on page 15, choose the area where you see the most design possibilities. Using a ruler and chalk marker, mark the area you want to use, keeping in mind that the design area should be 20½" x 34½".

2. Put your artist heart and eye into action. Stand back and start hunting for hidden treasures of flowers or whatever design you see. Remember this is about freedom.

3. Using a permanent marker that will show up on all colors, trace around all the designs you have selected. Keep in mind that the quilt is based on a small-scale fabric design, so if you make the designs too large, they will throw off the balance of the overall design.

4. Using a ruler and rotary cutter, trim the quilt center to 20½" x 34½".

5. Using the 1½"-wide inner border strips, trim one strip to measure 34½" long. Sew the strip to the right side of the quilt top. Measure the width of the quilt top; trim one strip to this length and sew it to the bottom of the quilt. Measure the length of the quilt; trim one strip to this length and sew it to the left side of the quilt. Measure the width again; trim the remaining strip to this length and sew it to the top of the quilt. Press all seam allowances open, referring to "Pressing" on page 24 for details.

6. Measure, trim, and sew the 4½"-wide outer-border strips to the quilt top in the same manner as for the inner border strips.

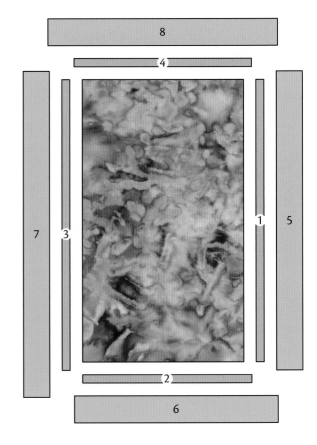

QUILTING

1. Refer to "Basting" on page 25. Layer the quilt top with backing and batting; baste.

2. Refer to "Free-Motion Quilting" on page 25. Using the 12-weight cotton thread, outline stitch around each marked design. Be sure to press after completing each design area so that puckers and tucks will not make this an "Oh no, I goofed!" process. Don't skip this step or you will create problems later during the quilting.

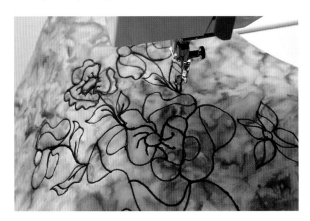

3. Using your chosen variegated thread, quilt inside the outlined flowers and leaves. Press after quilting each area.

4. Mark the feather quilting designs using a light chalk line as your guide. Keep the feathers in scale with the flowers and other designs.

5. Quilt the marked feathers and any other designs you wish to add.

FINISHING

Refer to "Finishing Your Art Quilt" on page 34 for details as needed.

1. Square up your quilt, trimming the outer border to 3¼" wide.

2. Add a hanging sleeve, if desired.

3. Using the 2½"-wide strips, sew the binding to the quilt.

PAINTING AND EMBELLISHING

1. Refer to "Painting on Fabric" on page 36. Paint the flowers, leaves, and feather motifs. Remember to let the paint dry between layers and before heat setting.

2. Refer to "Embellishments" on page 40. Sew beads, buttons, and other embellishments to the flowers, leaves, and background as desired. Add hot-fix crystals for accents.

3. Add a label.

FLORAL EXPLOSION
WALL QUILT

Big, bright, and bold—that's
what this project is all about! Working
on a larger scale doesn't necessarily mean creating
a larger quilt. This project guides you in working on
a large-scale floral project. As I was discovering my
hidden treasures in the fabric, thoughts of flowers
bursting out of the fabric ran through my mind.
I envisioned fireworks. So I grabbed the nearest
piece of paper, wrote "Floral Explosion" on it, and
stuck it on my design wall. The thought of fireworks
changed my entire view of the fabric. This time
my eyes did not initially see what my mind had
conceived. So remember, your mind is an artistic
tool. Develop it and you may find yourself going
beyond what you expected.

Finished size: 52½" x 44½"

MATERIALS

Yardage is based on 42"-wide fabric.

1½ yards of large-scale bright batik or hand-dyed fabric for quilt center

1 yard of fabric for outer border

⅓ yard of fabric for inner border

½ yard of fabric for binding

3⅛ yards of dark fabric for backing

60" x 52" piece of batting

12-weight dark cotton thread for outlining flowers

40-weight rayon or cotton variegated thread to match and enhance flowers

50-weight cotton thread for bobbin

Fabric paints

Hot-fix crystals, buttons, beads, and other embellishments

Chalk marker

Permanent marker

CUTTING

From the large-scale bright batik or hand-dyed fabric, cut:
1 piece, 49" x 42"

From the inner-border fabric, cut:
5 strips, 2" x 42"

From the outer-border fabric, cut:
5 strips, 6" x 42"

From the binding fabric, cut:
5 strips, 2½" x 42"

Designed and quilted by Judi Dains

ARTISTIC DESIGN SELECTION

1. Place the batik or hand-dyed quilt center on your design wall. Referring to "Finding and Marking the Designs" on page 15, stand back and look through a camera lens or reducing glass. This will help you see your design possibilities. Using a ruler and a chalk marker, mark the area you want to use, keeping in mind that the design area should be about 44½" x 36½".

2. Now is the time to let your imagination go wild. Start hunting for your "explosive" flowers. Keep in mind that you're working on large-scale objects, so keep the scale of the flowers true to the scale of the fabric. Flowers and objects should be larger than life. You may want to first mark your designs with chalk.

3. When you're sure you have the designs you want, use a permanent marker that will show up on all colors and trace around all the designs you've selected.

4. When working with large-scale designs, be aware of spatial constraints. Be careful not to overcrowd or bunch up your arrangement. Leave room for your quilting design.

5. Using a ruler and rotary cutter, trim the quilt center to 44½" x 36½".

6. Sew the 2"-wide inner-border strips together end to end to make a long strip. Measure the width of the quilt top. From the long strip, cut two strips to this length and sew them to the top and bottom of the quilt. Measure the length of the quilt. From the remaining strip, cut two strips to this length and sew them to the sides of the quilt. Press all seam allowances open, referring to "Pressing" on page 24 for details.

7. Sew the 6"-wide outer-border strips together end to end to make a long strip. Measure the length of the quilt top; cut one strip (from the long strip) and sew it to the left side of the quilt top. Measure the width of the quilt top; cut one strip to this length and sew it to the top of the quilt. Measure the length of the quilt; cut one strip to this length and sew it to the right side of the quilt. Measure the width again; trim the remaining strip to this length and sew it to the bottom of the quilt. Press all seam allowances open.

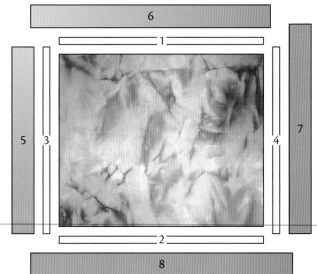

QUILTING

1. Refer to "Basting" on page 25. Layer the quilt top with backing and batting; baste.

2. Refer to "Free-Motion Quilting" on page 25. Using the 12-weight cotton thread, outline stitch around each marked design. Be sure to press after completing each design area to avoid puckers and tucks.

3. Using your chosen variegated thread, quilt inside the outlined objects. Press after quilting each area.

4. Mark the feather quilting designs using a light chalk line as your guide. Keep the feathers in scale with the flowers and other designs.

5. Quilt the marked feathers and any other designs you wish to add.

FINISHING

Refer to "Finishing Your Art Quilt" on page 34 for details as needed.

1. Square up your quilt, trimming the outer border to 5" wide.

2. Add a hanging sleeve, if desired.

3. Using the 2½"-wide strips, sew the binding to the quilt.

PAINTING AND EMBELLISHING

1. Refer to "Painting on Fabric" on page 36. Paint the flowers, leaves, and feather motifs. Remember to let the paint dry between layers and before heat setting.

2. Refer to "Embellishments" on page 40. Sew beads, buttons, and other embellishments to the flowers, leaves, and background as desired. Add hot-fix crystals for accents.

3. Add a label.

DOT, DOT, DOT
WALL ART

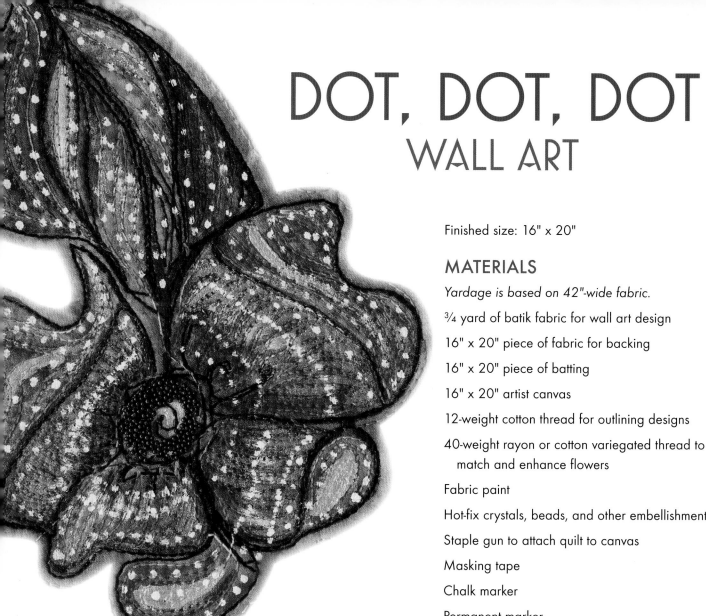

Finished size: 16" x 20"

MATERIALS

Yardage is based on 42"-wide fabric.

¾ yard of batik fabric for wall art design

16" x 20" piece of fabric for backing

16" x 20" piece of batting

16" x 20" artist canvas

12-weight cotton thread for outlining designs

40-weight rayon or cotton variegated thread to
    match and enhance flowers

Fabric paint

Hot-fix crystals, beads, and other embellishments

Staple gun to attach quilt to canvas

Masking tape

Chalk marker

Permanent marker

Quilts, even those that are wall-sized, can create an issue with how and where to hang them. An artist in one of my gallery showings suggested I make them on canvas. Canvas quilts have many advantages: you never have to worry about the quilting stitches on the back, and you don't have to use a good backing fabric because it isn't visible. The projects can be made in a matter of hours; a more detailed design may take a day. Wall art is easy to hang or frame, since frames are made to fit the canvas size. There is no binding or label to fuss with. I just sign the back of the canvas. You can get a large selection of canvas sizes already stretched on a wooden frame, so the frame won't warp on you and there's no blocking. They make excellent gifts. Now you can give all your family and friends a little piece of your artwork without much expense or time involved.

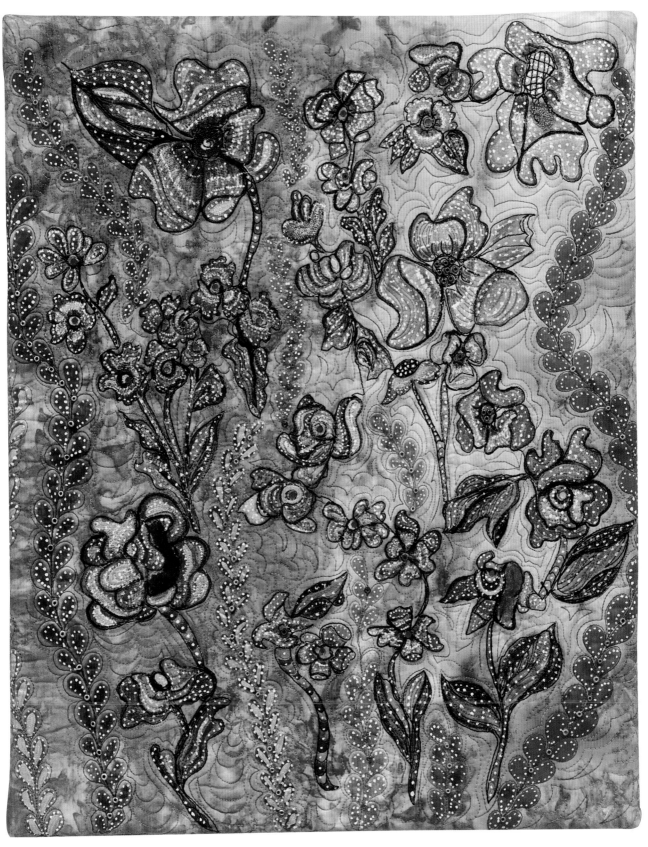

Designed and quilted by Judi Dains

ARTISTIC DESIGN SELECTION

1. Place the batik fabric on your design wall. Referring to "Finding and Marking the Designs" on page 15, choose the area where you see the most design possibilities. Using a ruler and chalk marker, mark the area you want to use, keeping in mind that the design area should be 16" x 20".

2. Put your artist heart and eye into action. Stand back and start hunting for hidden treasures of flowers or whatever design you see. Using a permanent marker that will show up on all colors, trace around all the designs you have selected.

3. Using a ruler and rotary cutter, trim the batik fabric to 22" x 26".

QUILTING

1. Refer to "Basting" on page 25. Place the backing and batting in the center of the wrong side of the batik fabric; baste. For this project, the batting and backing are cut *smaller* than the top fabric. The extra fabric is left unquilted so it can be wrapped around the artist canvas.

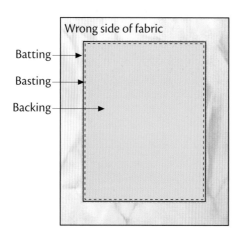

2. Refer to "Free-Motion Quilting" on page 25. Using the 12-weight cotton thread, outline stitch around each marked design. Be sure to press after completing each design area to avoid puckers and tucks.

3. Using your chosen variegated thread, quilt inside the outlined objects. Press after quilting each area.

4. Mark the feather quilting designs using a light chalk line as your guide. Keep the feathers in scale with the flowers and other designs.

5. Quilt the marked feathers and any other designs you wish to add. You'll only need to quilt the batik fabric in the marked 16" x 20" design area.

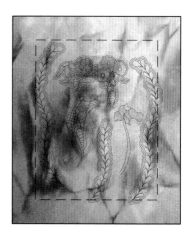

PAINTING AND EMBELLISHING

1. Refer to "Painting on Fabric" on page 36. Paint the flowers, leaves, and feather motifs. Remember to let the paint dry between layers and before heat setting.

2. Refer to "Embellishments" on page 40. Sew beads, buttons, and other embellishments to the flowers, leaves, and background as desired. Wait to affix any hot-fix crystals or other glued embellishments until the quilt is stapled to the artist canvas.

FINISHING

1. Center the artist canvas on the back of the quilt. Along the top, wrap the batik fabric over the edge of the artist canvas and fold the raw edge under. Tape the fabric to the board to temporarily hold it in place. Making sure the quilt is still centered, wrap the batik fabric over the bottom edge of the

artist canvas, folding under the raw edge, and tape it to the board. Make sure the quilt is centered, adjust if necessary, and staple along the top and bottom edges. Remove the tape.

Back of canvas

2. Repeat step 1 to wrap and staple the side edges to the back of the artist canvas.

3. Add hot-fix crystals and other glued embellishments. Sign your piece of art.

JUDI'S STYLIN'
BAG

Now I invite you to move from the role of quilt-maker to that of fashion designer. This pattern is basic and simple. It's up to you to make it yummy. Make a bag to match your favorite outfit or make it just to turn heads. The brighter the fabric, the better the bag.

Bags come in all shapes and sizes. For your convenience, I have designed a basic bag pattern. It will showcase your talent and make your friends green with envy. If you prefer to use another pattern, I encourage you to do so.

Finished dimension: 10" x 15" (not including handles)

MATERIALS

Yardage is based on 42"-wide fabric.

¾ yard of bright batik for front and back of bag

½ yard of muslin for backing

½ yard of fabric for lining

22" x 25" piece of fusible batting

2 wooden rings, 5" across, for bag handles

12-weight cotton thread for outlining designs

40-weight rayon or cotton variegated thread to match and enhance flowers

Tracing paper

Twin needle, size 2.0/80

Fabric paints

Hot-fix crystals, buttons, beads, and other embellishments

Magnetic clasp (optional)

Chalk marker

Permanent marker

Designed and quilted by Judi Dains

Back of bag

ARTISTIC DESIGN SELECTION

1. Enlarge and trace the outline of the bag pattern on page 64 onto a piece of tracing paper to make a paper template.

2. Place the batik fabric on your design wall. Referring to "Finding and Marking the Designs" on page 15, choose the area where you see the most design possibilities. You'll need to select two areas, one for each side of the bag, using the paper template to help determine the size of the areas.

3. Place the paper template over one chosen design area, and using chalk, trace the exact shape of the template onto the fabric. Make one bag front and one bag back.

4. Trim the excess fabric, leaving at least 1" beyond the marked lines on all sides. You'll be able to hold onto this extra fabric when quilting.

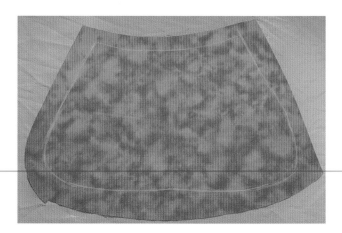

5. Using a permanent marker that will show up on all colors, trace around all the designs you have selected.

QUILTING AND PAINTING THE BAG

1. Cut two pieces of muslin backing and two pieces of batting the same size as the batik bag pieces. Following the manufacturer's directions, fuse the bag front, batting, and backing together. Repeat to fuse the bag back, batting, and backing.

2. Refer to "Free-Motion Quilting" on page 25. Using the 12-weight cotton thread, outline stitch around each marked design. Be sure to press after completing each design area to avoid puckers and tucks.

3. Trim the excess fabric and batting from the bag front and back pieces, cutting on the marked chalk line. If your chalk line has disappeared, use the paper template to re-mark the lines.

4. Refer to "Painting on Fabric" on page 36. Paint the flowers, leaves, and feather motifs. Remember to let the paint dry between layers and before heat setting.

MAKING THE BAG YOKE

1. Trace the outline of the yoke pattern on page 65 onto a piece of tracing paper to make a paper template.

2. Cut four 6" x 11" batik pieces. Using the yoke paper template and chalk, trace the exact shape of the template onto each batik piece. Use a ruler and chalk to draw diagonal lines creating a cross-hatch design on each piece. Using a twin needle, position the needle over the line so that the marked line is centered between the needles; stitch on each chalk line. Make a total of four pieces.

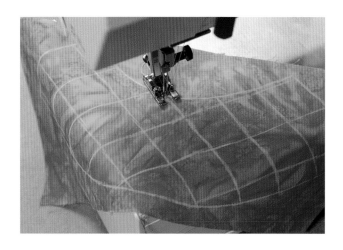

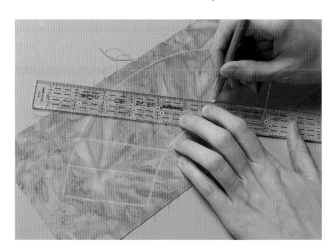

Using a Twin Needle

First replace your regular sewing machine needle with a twin needle (also called a double needle). Make sure you're using your regular needle plate, not a single-hole or straight-stitch needle plate. You will need to thread your machine with two threads for this process. Place the threads in the thread holders with one spool in the position closest to the tension and the second spool somewhere behind the first one. Taking both threads in your hand, bring them through the upper-thread tension dial together, placing a thread on each side of the tension dial. Thread the needle on the left with the first thread, and then thread the needle on the right with the second thread.

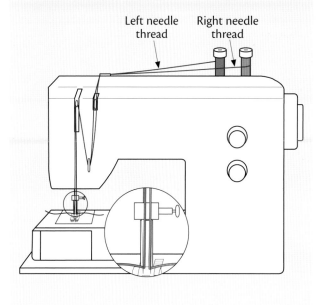

Left needle thread   Right needle thread

3. Trim the excess fabric from the yoke pieces, cutting on the outside chalk line. If your chalk line has disappeared, use the paper template to re-mark the line.

4. Using the paper template, cut two pieces of batting. Fuse the batting to the wrong side of two of the yoke pieces from step 3.

5. With right sides together, sew one yoke piece from step 3 and one yoke piece from step 4 together along the inner curved edge as shown, using a ⅝"-wide seam allowance. Clip the seam allowances. Make two.

6. Use the paper template to cut four pieces from the lining fabric. With right sides together and using a ⅝"-wide seam allowance, sew two lining pieces together along the inner curved edge in the same manner. Make two.

ASSEMBLING THE BAG

1. With right sides together, sew the bag front and back together, using a ⅝"-wide seam allowance and backstitching at the top edge as shown. Along the top edge, turn the ⅝"-wide seam allowance under and press.

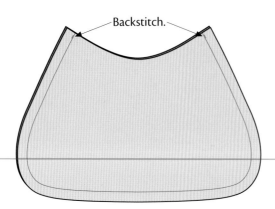

Backstitch.

2. Place one batik yoke and one lining yoke right sides together and sew along both side edges using a ⅝"-wide seam allowance. Make two. Clip the seam allowances and turn the units right side out.

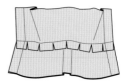

3. Fold a yoke from step 2 over each handle as shown and baste the raw edges together.

4. Position the folded edge of the bag front on top of a yoke from step 3. Topstitch in place as shown. Topstitch the bag back to the remaining yoke.

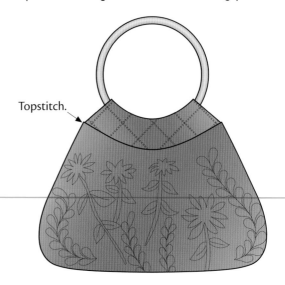

Topstitch.

5. Using the bag template, cut two pieces from the lining fabric. Repeat step 1 to sew the two lining pieces together. Along the top edge, turn the ⅝"-wide seam allowance under and press.

6. Place the lining inside the bag, wrong sides together, so that the folded edge of the lining covers the raw edges and stitching line on the yoke. Hand stitch in place.

7. Refer to "Embellishments" on page 40. Sew beads, buttons, and other embellishments to the flowers, leaves, and background, as desired. Add hot-fix crystals for accents. Attach a magnetic clasp, if desired, following the manufacturer's instructions.

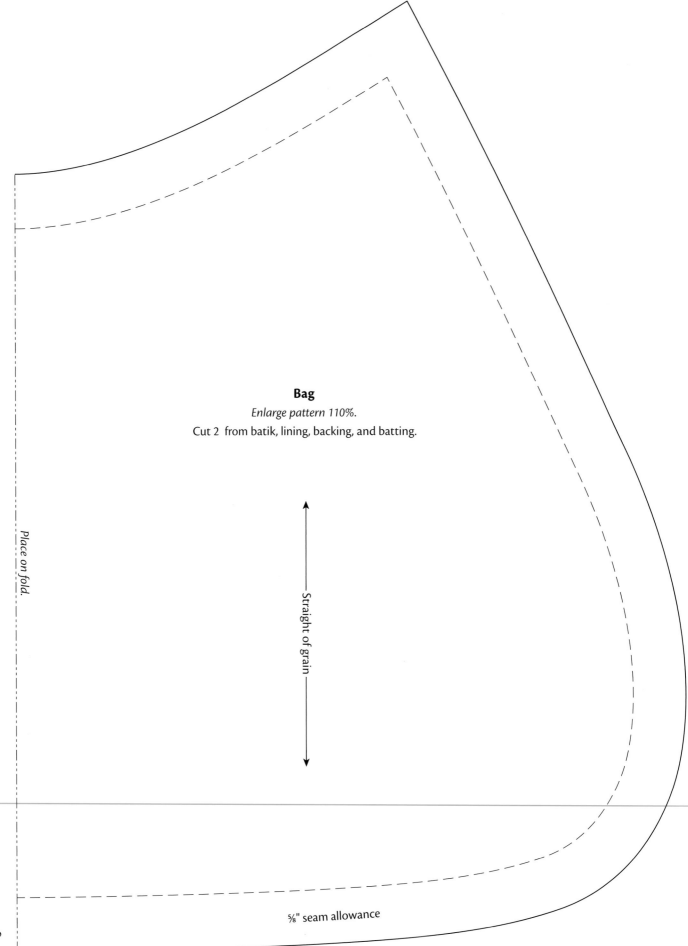

Bag

Enlarge pattern 110%.

Cut 2 from batik, lining, backing, and batting.

Place on fold.

Straight of grain

⅝" seam allowance

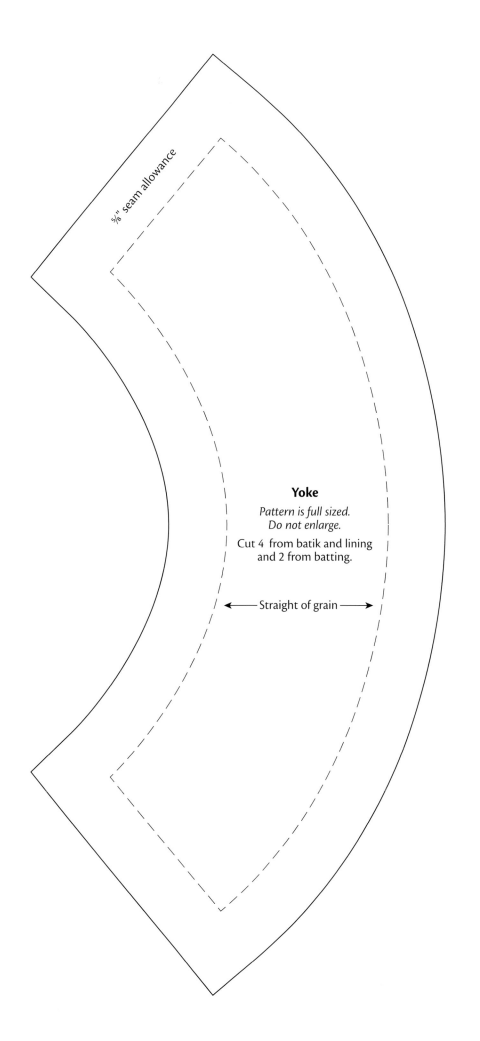

5/8" seam allowance

Yoke

Pattern is full sized.
Do not enlarge.

Cut 4 from batik and lining
and 2 from batting.

←——— Straight of grain ———→

DECORATIVE
PILLOW

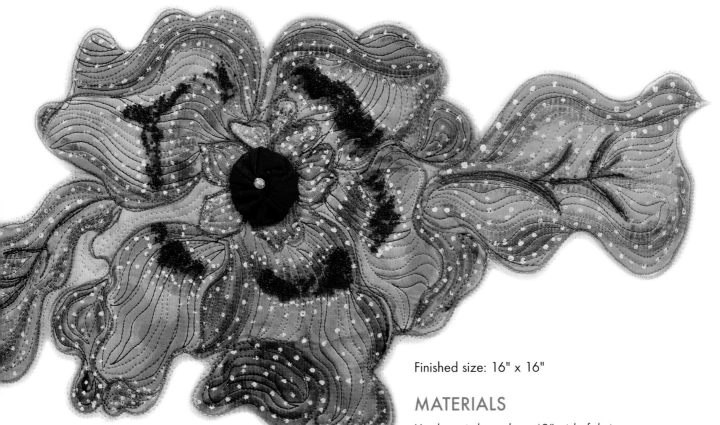

In today's world, a great pillow speaks volumes. Decorators use them to change the atmosphere in a room. In fact, pillows are a most sought-after designer item. They come in all sizes, shapes, colors, and materials and can be very costly. For this project I used one great batik fabric and did a different design on each side. Quilters have a wonderful range of batik fabrics available, which makes it enjoyable to find just the right one to fit our decor.

Finished size: 16" x 16"

MATERIALS

Yardage is based on 42"-wide fabric.

1 yard of batik fabric for pillow front, back, and bias piping

⅝ yard of muslin for pillow lining

2 pieces, 18" x 18", of batting for pillow

12-weight dark cotton thread for outlining flowers

40-weight rayon or cotton variegated thread to match and enhance flowers

2½ yards of ¼"-diameter cotton cording for piping

Fabric paints

Hot-fix crystals, buttons, beads, and other embellishments

16" x 16" pillow form

Zipper or hook-and-eye tape (optional)

Chalk marker

Permanent marker

Designed and quilted by Judi Dains

ARTISTIC DESIGN SELECTION

1. Place the batik fabric on your design wall. Referring to "Finding and Marking the Designs" on page 15, choose the area where you see the most design possibilities. Using a ruler and chalk marker, mark the 16" x 16" design area you want to use. For this small project, you'll only need to allow 2" on all sides of the area for quilting rather than the usual 4". Select two design areas, one for the pillow front and one for the pillow back.

2. Put your artist heart and eye into action. Stand back and start hunting for hidden treasures of flowers or whatever design you see. Make sure your design falls in the center of the pillow; if it's too close to the edge, some of the design might be lost. Using a permanent marker that will show up on all colors, trace around all the designs you have selected.

3. Using a ruler and rotary cutter, trim each design area to 18" x 18".

QUILTING

1. Cut two 18" x 18" squares of muslin.

2. Refer to "Basting" on page 25. Layer the pillow top with a muslin square and batting; baste. Repeat for the pillow back.

3. Refer to "Free-Motion Quilting" on page 25. Using the 12-weight cotton thread, outline stitch around each marked design. Be sure to press after completing each design area to avoid puckers and tucks.

4. Using your chosen variegated thread, quilt inside the outlined objects. Press after quilting each area.

5. Mark the feather quilting designs using a light chalk line as your guide. Keep the feathers in scale with the flowers and other designs.

6. Quilt the marked feathers and any other designs you wish to add.

PAINTING AND EMBELLISHING

1. Refer to "Painting on Fabric" on page 36. Paint the flowers, leaves, and feather motifs. Remember to let the paint dry between layers and before heat setting.

2. Refer to "Embellishments" on page 40. Sew beads and buttons to the flowers, leaves, and background as desired. Wait to sew on yo-yos or to affix any hot-fix crystals or other glued embellishments until the pillow is finished.

FINISHING THE PILLOW

1. Trim the pillow front, muslin, and batting to 16½" x 16½". Be sure to trim an equal amount from all sides so that the design area is centered in the square. Repeat to trim the pillow back.

2. Refer to "Covering Cording" on page 69 to make the piping.

3. Align the raw edges of the pillow front and piping. Sew the piping around the edge of the pillow front with a ¼"-wide seam allowance. Start in the middle of the bottom edge and stitch around the pillow, overlapping the beginning and ending tails of the piping as shown. Stitch across the piping where the tails cross. Trim the ends of the piping even with the raw edge of the pillow front.

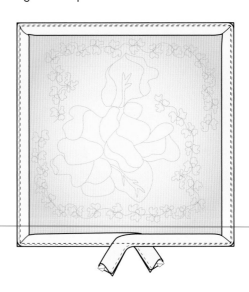

Note: If you plan to use a zipper or hook-and-loop tape, you will need to sew them to the pillow before proceeding to step 4. Be sure to follow the manufacturer's instructions for the product you are using.

4. With the pillow front on top, place the front and back of the pillow right sides together and sew around the edges with a ¼"-wide seam allowance.

Leave an 8" to 10" opening to turn the pillow right side out. Backstitch on each side of the opening.

5. Turn the pillow right side out. Insert the pillow form and close the opening with a slip stitch.

6. Embellish as desired. You may want to add yo-yos, hot-fix crystals, micro beads, and other embellishments.

Covering Cording

1. Cut about 80" of 2"-wide bias strips.

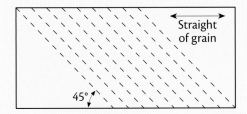

2. Sew the strips together end to end and press the seam allowances open.

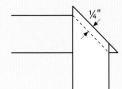

3. To cover the cording, fold the fabric strip in half lengthwise, wrong sides together. Insert the cording, pushing it snugly against the fold.

4. Use a zipper foot on your sewing machine and set the needle so that it sews to the left of the foot. (Be sure to use a regular needle plate, not a single-hole needle plate.) Sew the two edges of the fabric together, enclosing the cording.

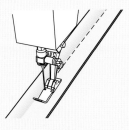

5. When you've enclosed the entire piece of cording, trim the seam allowance evenly to ¼".

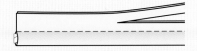

GALLERY

For the past few years I've been working on the body of work that I've shared with you in this book. In the gallery section, I've gathered some of my quilts and projects that successfully use different types of batiks. There is so much more to exploring the possibilities that are hidden in those wonderful batik and hand-dyed fabrics. As I selected projects for the gallery, I saw even more possibilities. This is a technique that will grow on you and keep you enthused as you, too, explore more and more ways to work with the batiks, paints, inks, and painting tools. The caption for each quilt may help you see more clearly the different ways you can work with your chosen fabrics.

Dragonfly Swarm, 28" x 39", by Judi Dains

This was a batik with large yet very subtle color changes. Leaves and flowers that are large and close together consume most of the batik fabrics. Little dragonflies of micro-bead origin swarm through the sparkling nail heads and crystals. Fabric paint and ink worked well on the silk dupioni borders. I only used one ink color in the borders, yet the ink looks different on each color because it absorbs and reacts differently on each silk, which makes yet another unplanned design element.

Kathy's Creation, 28" x 47", by Kathy Sanchez, Grass Valley, California

Kathy was a student in one of my workshops. She used a Phil Beaver fabric in bright yellow and brown colors and chose to make large leaves and flowers to overpower the brightness of her fabric. She used watered-down Jacquard Lumiere paint to get the desired effects in the leaves and flowers, which also gives the borders a gilded look.

The Vineyard, 37" x 50", by Judi Dains

This batik had large color splashes. The grape theme seemed to be ready-made for me. It's embellished with crystals, giving the grapes a fresh-morning-dew look. The back of this quilt is equally exquisite and is shown on page 23.

Walk through My Garden, 27½" x 47", by Judi Dains

This piece is more like a watercolor painting than any of my other pieces. I experimented with the Tsukineko All-Purpose Inks by watering them down and letting them run, and I was very pleased with the results.

**Delightful Posies,
17" x 46", by Judi Dains**

This design was made from a tie-dyed batik. The flower placement covers the batik's burst of lime color, hiding most of the lime color in the batik. This changes the look of the background colors to show more of the pink and blue shades. I chose the lime and apple green borders based on the lime green beneath the flowers. Since the colors are in the batik, they blend with the pinks and blues that show in the background.

**Autumn Splendor,
17" x 43", by Judi Dains**

While I experimented with different fabric pens, paints, and ink processes, some of the products bled to the back of the quilt, which is orange. This could have been an obvious mistake. The pens were supposedly permanent; however, they weren't designed for fabric, and some of them ran when sprayed with water. Lesson learned: *stay with products designed for fabrics.* I tossed the quilt into the washer and dryer, and most of the colors on the back came out. The quilt also now had less color on the front, but it was brilliant and beautiful, and not one crystal was lost in the process.

**Whispering Flower,
19" x 50", by Judi Dains**

With this one I used only one color range for the flowers so that they would stand out. I chose orange for the flowers to blend with the orange color in the background of the batik. Adding a silk dupioni inner border that matched several colors in the batik brought the flowers out even more. The soft butter yellow outer borders were only partly painted. Sometimes it's just nice to have a place for the eye to rest! The colored feathers were done with several colors of fabric pens. The name came to me when I looked at the flower at the top of the quilt. It looked like it was bending down to speak in a soft voice to the other flowers below, and if you look at them, they look like they're leaning upward to hear what the whispering flower is saying!

**Delicate Beauties,
18" x 42", by Judi Dains**

This is the same batik fabric I used in "Whispering Flower" on page 78. This time I used several of the colors from the batik. What a difference paint and borders make! The inner border brings out the brilliance of the batik, while the outer, gradated border gives a tranquil effect.

Apple Core? 20" x 34", designed by Judi Dains

This tie-dyed fabric may have been from as far back as the 1980s. So check your stash! I chose to cover the large blotches on the fabric and keep the design of the dye marks as close as possible to what they were originally. This quilt design came out almost abstract. The design on the middle right reminds me of an apple core. I used Jacquard Lumiere and other paints. The painted dots bring this piece to life.

Blowing in the Wind, 53" x 22", by Judi Dains

I balanced the dark batik fabric by heavily outlining and accenting the leaves and flowers with fabric pens, leaving the centers of the leaves and flowers almost devoid of paint. The feathers were all done with fabric pens. A light glittering of crystals shine just enough to add spark, yet not enough to overpower the batik.

**Brenda's Gift,
14" x 22", by Judi Dains;**

from the collection of Brenda Miller,
Fair Oaks, California

The center batik is a preprinted fabric
with butterflies already stamped on the
fabric. I usually avoid this type of batik,
but I decided to use the butterflies as
part of my design by adding three large
flowers around the butterflies. The paint
on the inner border of Fairy Frost by
Michael Miller Fabrics shows up beautifully. The outer border is silk dupioni.

My Beautiful Garden, 16" x 20", by Judi Dains

This was a very bright batik, so I had to go over and over the colors to make them show up on the powerful fabric. I used fabric pens for almost all the flowers. As I painted, the colors looked bright, but by the next day they had faded into the fibers. I kept going back over them each day until I was satisfied. They have stayed their beautiful brilliant color.

Tuscany Gold
(front view), 25" x 50",
by Judi Dains

This subtle brown-and-olive batik
challenged me. It took me a while
to figure out what colors to paint
the flowers. I chose various colors,
using many combinations of fabric
ink, paint, and pens. The feathers in
the border are painted with metallic
Jacquard paint. I added white paint
as a dotted accent to give the quilt
a Mediterranean-inspired look. It's
heavily embellished with crystals,
nail-head tins, micro-beaded bees,
and butterflies.

Tuscany Gold (back view)

The back of the quilt shows the exquisite quilting. I used a 100-weight soft gold silk thread on the top and in the bobbin because I didn't want the quilting stitches on the quilt front to take away from the great fabric or the flowers. To quilt inside the flowers, I used a 100-weight lavender silk thread.

**Under the Sea, 22" x 38",
by Judi Dains**

The center tie-dyed fabric was probably from the 1980s and was buried deep in my stash. To me it looked like the rays of the sun shining down through the water, giving me a glimpse of life under the sea. The red dot at the top was part of the fabric, but I colored it brighter. The black marks at the side were also part of the fabric and reminded me of shadows or seaweed. I did very little to this piece except to add kelp, sea urchins, fish, and a few other critters that might lurk under the sea. The first border of gold Fairy Frost fabric by Michael Miller Fabrics adds a nice shimmering effect. I painted the kelp in the border with fabric pens and then added glitz and glitter throughout.

Sea Life, 16" x 20", by Judi Dains

This was a questionable batik, what I categorize as a "muddy" batik. However, in smaller pieces it was okay to use. There were small circles in the fabric, so I added more small circles using a VersaCraft ink pad and a sponge dauber. Then I added the fish, coral, and underwater life. The embellishments include beads, crystals, and yo-yos.

Aquatic Sightings Jacket, by Judi Dains

This jacket is made from three batik fabrics, starting at the hem with the darkest batik and gradually moving up to the center with second batik to end with the lightest batik on top. I used a raw-edge appliqué technique for this piece and embellished it with paint, ink, beads, bangles, covered buttons, and crystals.

Back of jacket

The bodice of the satin dress has been quilted using Soft Touch batting, and then embellished with crystals to add just the right touch of sparkle.

"Beyond the Surface Lies a Hidden Garden" Jacket, by Judi Dains

This jacket is made from one piece of fabric using one of my favorite batik color waves. The colors softly and gradually shift from greens to yellows to pinks and lavenders. I cut out each pattern piece so that the two front pieces and the back would have the green at the bottom. The sleeves were cut so the sleeve opening would also have as much of the green as possible. This does take more fabric, and the amount depends on the repeat of the batik pattern. The jacket is embellished with beads, crystals, covered buttons, yo-yos, and micro beads.

Back of jacket

Hidden Garden Purse, by Judi Dains

Every ensemble needs the perfect purse. The leftover batik fabrics (from the jacket) were used to create this little sling purse. The techniques of quilting, painting, and embellishing used in the jacket were also used to create this little purse.

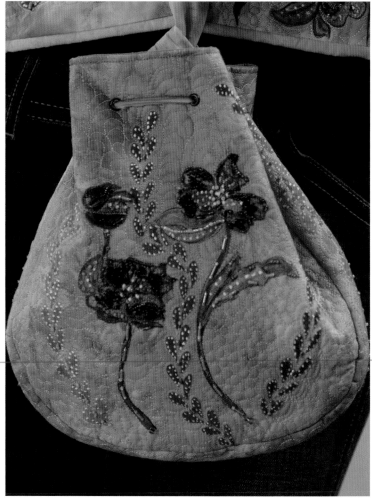

Aquatic Sightings Vest, by Judi Dains

The Aquatic Sightings jacket hides yet another sweet surprise. To carry on the theme, I made this vest. It has no quilting, paint, or sparkling crystals. The raw silk vest boasts raw-edge appliqué and designer yarns stitched with a couching method.

ABOUT THE AUTHOR

When Judi Dains was younger, if someone had told her that she would be a quiltmaker and a designer of wearable art, she would have laughed and maybe even disputed the issue. She was a content mother of two. Content? There wasn't a hobby or craft that got by her. From the earliest she can recall, she was busy with her hands and mind, creating with abandon.

As her children were growing up, Judi volunteered for everything that came her way. She became everything from PTA President to the first female baseball coach in her area to Girl Scout leader, and on and on. As life went on, she became involved with horses and motorcycles, and at the young age of 38, she took up competitive roller skating.

Quilting escaped her notice until the late 1980s. She kept envisioning wild clothes, only to find out that her visions were called wearable art. That is what led her into the quilt world, where her volunteering skills served her well. Judi served on two local quilt boards for 15 years, taking on many positions, including president and quilt-show chair.

Through the years, she has won more than 275 awards. Her work has been shown in galleries and public buildings, including the governor's office in California's State Capitol, where two of her quilts were on loan at the same time. Her work is in many private collections and hospitals, in the Assembly of God Headquarters in Greece, and in various other public places.

Judi has worked her quilting and wearable-art skills into her Heart of God Fashion Ministry, presenting the gospel to women's groups through her designs. She also teaches and lectures at quilt-related guilds.

She is blessed with two beautiful children, Cindy Stanley (Grace's mommy) and Brian Hubbard (the father of Adam, Marisa, and Cheyenne). Judi has been married to her husband, Jim, for 30 years, and they are both very active in their faith, still volunteering wherever needed.

NEW AND BEST-SELLING TITLES FROM

 America's Best-Loved
Quilt Books®

America's Best-Loved Craft & Hobby Books®
America's Best-Loved Knitting Books®

APPLIQUÉ
Appliqué Quilt Revival
Beautiful Blooms
Cutting-Garden Quilts
Dream Landscapes
Easy Appliqué Blocks—*NEW!*
Simple Comforts—*NEW!*
Sunbonnet Sue and Scottie Too

BABIES AND CHILDREN
Baby's First Quilts
Baby Wraps
Let's Pretend
The Little Box of Baby Quilts
Snuggle-and-Learn Quilts for Kids
Sweet and Simple Baby Quilts

BEGINNER
Color for the Terrified Quilter
Happy Endings, Revised Edition
Machine Appliqué for the Terrified Quilter
Your First Quilt Book (or it should be!)

GENERAL QUILTMAKING
Adventures in Circles
American Jane's Quilts for All Seasons
Bits and Pieces
Bold and Beautiful—*NEW!*
Cool Girls Quilt
Country-Fresh Quilts
Creating Your Perfect Quilting Space
**Fig Tree Quilts: Fresh Vintage Sewing—
*NEW!***
Folk-Art Favorites—*NEW!*
Follow-the-Line Quilting Designs
    Volume Three
Gathered from the Garden
The New Handmade
Points of View
Prairie Children and Their Quilts
Quilt Revival
A Quilter's Diary
Quilter's Happy Hour
Quilting for Joy
Remembering Adelia—*NEW!*
Sensational Sashiko

Simple Seasons
Skinny Quilts and Table Runners
**That Patchwork Place® Quilt Collection—
*NEW!***
Twice Quilted
Young at Heart Quilts

HOLIDAY AND SEASONAL
Christmas Quilts from Hopscotch
Comfort and Joy
Holiday Wrappings

HOOKED RUGS, NEEDLE FELTING, AND PUNCHNEEDLE
The Americana Collection
Miniature Punchneedle Embroidery
Needle-Felting Magic
Needle Felting with Cotton and Wool

PAPER PIECING
Easy Reversible Vests, Revised Edition
Paper-Pieced Mini Quilts
Show Me How to Paper Piece
Showstopping Quilts to Foundation Piece
A Year of Paper Piecing

PIECING
501 Rotary-Cut Quilt Blocks
Favorite Traditional Quilts Made Easy
Loose Change
Maple Leaf Quilts
Mosaic Picture Quilts
New Cuts for New Quilts
Nine by Nine
On-Point Quilts
Quiltastic Curves
Ribbon Star Quilts
Rolling Along

QUICK QUILTS
40 Fabulous Quick-Cut Quilts
Instant Bargello
Quilts on the Double
Sew Fun, Sew Colorful Quilts
Supersize 'Em!—*NEW!*

SCRAP QUILTS
Nickel Quilts
Save the Scraps
Scrap-Basket Surprises—*NEW!*
Simple Strategies for Scrap Quilts
Spotlight on Scraps

CRAFTS
A to Z of Sewing—*NEW!*
Art from the Heart
The Beader's Handbook
Card Design
Crochet for Beaders
Dolly Mama Beads
Embellished Memories
Friendship Bracelets All Grown Up
Making Beautiful Jewelry
Paper It!
Trading Card Treasures

KNITTING & CROCHET
365 Crochet Stitches a Year:
    Perpetual Calendar
365 Knitting Stitches a Year:
    Perpetual Calendar
A to Z of Knitting
All about Knitting
Amigurumi World
Beyond Wool
Cable Confidence
Casual, Elegant Knits
Crocheted Pursenalities
Gigi Knits…and Purls
Kitty Knits
Knitted Finger Puppets
The Knitter's Book of Finishing
    Techniques
Knitting Circles around Socks
Knitting with Gigi
More Sensational Knitted Socks
Pursenalities
Simple Stitches—*NEW!*
Toe-Up Techniques for Hand Knit
    Socks, Revised Edition
Together or Separate

Our books are available at bookstores and your favorite craft, fabric,
and yarn retailers. If you don't see the title you're looking for,
visit us at **www.martingale-pub.com** or contact us at:

1-800-426-3126
International: 1-425-483-3313
Fax: 1-425-486-7596 • **Email:** info@martingale-pub.com